July 5, 2011

Happ

Mавrик.

All our love + Best Wishes!

Papa & Gram

XO

WE WON THE CUP!

BOSTON BRUINS
2011 STANLEY CUP
CHAMPIONS

www.bostonherald.com

Boston Herald

Publisher
Patrick J. Purcell

Editor In Chief
Joe Sciacca

Sports Editor
Hank Hryniewicz

Photo Editor
Jim Mahoney

Photo Contributors
Stuart Cahill
Christopher Evans
Matt Stone
Matthew West

Project Editor
Paul Gaeta

Contributing Writers
Ron Borges
Steve Buckley
Steve Conroy
Dan Duggan
Stephen Harris
Matt Kalman
Rich Thompson

Special Thanks:
Bill McIlwrath, Mark Murphy, Joe Thomas and the Boston Herald copy desk

KCI Sports Publishing
Publisher
Peter J. Clark
Managing Editor
Molly Voorheis
Book and Cover Design
Nicky Brillowski

ISBN: 978-0-9831985-9-8 (PB)
ISBN: 978-0-9831985-3-6 (HC)

Printed in the United States of America
KCI Sports Publishing   3340 Whiting Avenue, Suite 5   Stevens Point, WI 54481
Phone: 1-800-697-3756   Fax: 715-344-2668
www.kcisports.com

The City of Boston has certainly turned into a city of champions over the past decade.

So with a boatload of memories over the past 10 years of celebratory Rolling Rallies with champion-filled Duck Boats weaving through mobs of cheering fans lining the city's streets, we welcome the 2010-11 Bruins to the party!

These Bruins get to take over the spotlight from the Patriots (2001, 2003, 2004), the Red Sox (2004 and 2007) and the Celtics (2008). It's been 39 years since Bobby Orr and the Big, Bad Bruins took our city by storm and brought the Stanley Cup home to a place where the streets are paved with Black 'n' Gold.

Above: *Bruins defenseman Johnny Boychuk (55) and goalie Tim Thomas (30) enjoy the moment as Rich Peverley comes in after the team finished off Vancouver in Game 7 of the Stanley Cup finals.* Christopher Evans | Boston Herald

It's been a long wait for Bruins Nation, but every card-carrying member will tell you it's been worth the wait!

In all of that time — through the remainder of the '70s, when the Bruins flirted with the Cup in '74, '77 and '78; on through the '80s when they could taste it again in '88 and '90 only to be quieted by the Edmonton Oilers in the finals; and even when beloved captain Ray Bourque left town in one last lunge for the Cup and took it home with the Colorado Avalanche in 2001 — this city and its hockey faithful never gave up hope.

That faith in the Bruins and the team's gritty, tough-as-nails approach of out-working, out-hitting and out-hustling its opponents has been rewarded once again. The Cup is back! The passionate fandom never left! Let the celebration begin!

In these pages, the Boston Herald proudly brings you on a trip down memory lane through the Bruins' playoff run that came to its jubilant conclusion in Game 7 against the Canucks in the Great Northwest. Use this keepsake as a compass, carrying you along the path of the champion Bruins. Our award-winning photographers give you the best view in the house of all the ups and downs through the playoffs. Our stable of hard-working beat writers and columnists give you an inside look at the incredible journey that brought Lord Stanley's Cup back to Boston.

Celebrate this season and save this book to revisit the Bruins' magical moments and the hard-working, hard-hitting and hard-to-forget players both stars and role guys — who rewarded our faith in the Black 'n' Gold by climbing back to the top of the heap in the NHL.

Welcome back Bruins! Let's do it again some time soon.■

Above: Fans at the Garden erupt after Nathan Horton's third-period goal against Tampa Bay put the Bruins up 1-0 in Game 7 of the Eastern Conference finals. Christopher Evans |Boston Herald

CONTENTS

CANADIENS 2 / BRUINS 0

EASTERN CONFERENCE QUARTERFINALS   GAME 1   4-14-11

By Steve Conroy

Above: *The Bruins flag is hoisted in the air by fans prior to Game 1 against Montreal at the Garden.*
Matt Stone | Boston Herald

Anyone expecting the Bruins to trample over Montreal as they did in the Canadiens' last two trips to the Garden had a very cold bucket of reality dumped on them last night.

In Game 1 of the Eastern Conference quarterfinals on Causeway Street, the Canadiens scored in the opening minutes and then added a late goal for a 2-0 victory against the Bruins and a 1-0 lead in the best-of-seven series.

The B's worked for 82 games to earn home-ice advantage in this series, and now it's in the hands of the Canadiens.

Brian Gionta scored the Montreal goals, both coming on defensive-zone turnovers by the Bruins. Carey Price stopped all 31 shots the hosts threw at him.

The Bruins at times dominated territorially, especially in the second period when they outshot the Habs 18-6, but they didn't make Price's job hard enough. He posted his third playoff shutout, all of which have come at the Bruins' expense.

"We were all around the net, we just weren't in front of it. That's something that we have to get better," B's coach Claude Julien said.

The Canadiens followed the blueprint they used last postseason to upset Washington and Pittsburgh on their way to the conference finals. And the first rule of that template is to score the first goal, which they did just 2:44 into the game.

Tomas Kaberle fired a hard backhanded pass behind his net that was too hot for partner Dennis Seidenberg to handle, and it went to Montreal's Scott Gomez along the left wall. Gomez then zipped a pass down to Gionta at the right side of the net, and the Montreal captain beat Tim Thomas on a shot he had little chance to stop.

"I (passed it) too hard," Kaberle said. "That wasn't the plan, and it ended up on Gomez' stick."

From that point until the third period, the Bruins had waves of momentum and Kaberle

Above: *Bruins right winger Nathan Horton dives over Montreal goalie Carey Price during the first period of Game 1 at the Garden.*
Matt Stone | Boston Herald

had a couple of chances to atone for his mistake when he made two great passes to set up Brad Marchand. The first came on the Bruins' first power-play opportunity (0-for-3 on the night) as Kaberle sent Marchand off on a clean break-in. Marchand made a nice move to his backhand, but he couldn't lift it over Price's left pad. The next one looked like a gift-wrapped goal for the rookie late in the first. Kaberle fired a terrific pass from the left point to Marchand for a backdoor goal but, with half the net staring at him, he heeled the puck

and it went to the end boards.

"It was a perfect pass," Marchand said. "I rushed it a bit. I should have tried to stop it and I would have had a wide-open net. But I just rushed it a bit."

Every missed opportunity can come back to haunt you in the playoffs, and those were two right there. The B's had a lot more in the second period, when Price was at his best.

But the Canadiens weathered that storm and played a much better third period, limiting the Bruins to five shots while the Montreal

Above: *Montreal right winger Brian Gionta celebrates after scoring on Bruins goalie Tim Thomas during the first period of Game 1 at the Garden.*
Matt Stone | Boston Herald

defensive pair of Hal Gill and P.K. Subban did a good job of shutting down the top line of Milan Lucic, David Krejci and Nathan Horton.

With the B's pressing for the equalizer, Gomez stole the puck from Lucic as the forward was trying to break out of the zone. He fed it over to Gionta, whose shot broke through Thomas and into the net.

"I was trying to beat (Gomez)," Lucic said. "I created a lot of speed and he was kind of standing still, and I was trying to go around him. He did a really good job of reading what I was going to do and he created a turnover. And they got a goal. I can't let that get to me.

I can't let that affect my play. I still got to go out there and do what I do and sometimes it is carrying the puck through the neutral zone."

Now, with just one playoff game under their belts, the Bruins are looking at a must-win game here tomorrow night before heading to Montreal for Games 3 and 4. It may not be panic time for the B's just yet, but it creeps up awfully quickly in the postseason.

"It's not a secret," Lucic said. "The Bell Centre is not an easy building for us to win in, especially this year, and it's definitely a must-win (tomorrow) to try to get the split."∎

By Steve Buckley

A couple of days ago, Bruins general manager Peter Chiarelli was asked how far his team needs to advance in the postseason in order for this season to be stamped a success.

When Chiarelli offered a roundabout response that "the obvious answer is to get past the second round," a lot of B's fans rightly squawked that the team's only goal should be to win the Stanley Cup.

Make it past the second round?

Win the Stanley Cup?

After what happened last night at the Garden, a better question might be: Will this be another postseason in which the Bruins don't even get out of the first round?

For in spite of all the good cheer and optimism as they entered the playoffs, the Bruins came up empty last night at the Garden, dropping a 2-0 decision to the Montreal Canadiens in Game 1 of the Eastern Conference quarterfinals. If it's a silver lining you want, dig right in. The Bruins did outshoot the Habs, 31-20, which would suggest that they controlled the tempo but, alas, couldn't put a shot past goalie Carey Price.

But while Price absolutely deserved his shutout, let's not confuse him with Ken Dryden, 1971. The fact is that the Bruins got off to a sluggish start, fell behind early, were 0-for-3 on the power play and did not, as had been expected, outmuscle the Canadiens. Forget about intimidating the Habs. There wasn't a single fight last night, and only seven minor penalties — combined — were assessed by the officials.

So much for the Bruins using Game 1 to make a statement about where they are headed this postseason.

The Bruins' postgame mood was strange, and strained. When Zdeno Chara met with a crowd of reporters and the first question was a softball about how frustrated this team must feel, the B's captain replied by asking, "Who says we're frustrated? We just didn't score a goal. I think we did a lot of good things. We just didn't score a goal."

Memo No. 1 to Zdeno Chara: There's a pretty good chance that thousands of Bruins fans last night met the clinical definition of "frustrated." As for the big guy's claim that the Bruins "did a lot of good things," that's not going to go over well with the fans. He sounds like onetime Red Sox GM Dan Duquette putting a shine on a failed season by pointing out that the Sox had spent "more days in first place" than the pennant-winning Yankees.

And then there was Bruins goaltender Tim Thomas. Asked to explain Brian Gionta's first-period goal, the veteran goaltender paused for a beat and then said, "I'm not a play-by-play announcer."

Memo No. 2 to Zdeno Chara: Tim Thomas appeared to be "frustrated" by last night's loss.

"We did carry the play for the majority of the game," offered Thomas. "We just couldn't score ... and we didn't really penetrate to the areas that you need to score. We were close. We were trying. We just couldn't get there."

Sorry, Bruins fans, but some of this brings to mind Red Sox pitcher John Lackey ladling out a bowlful of excuses after his latest bow-wow pitching performance. Though there was, indeed, some tough talk to be found in the Bruins locker room — "We've got to make sure we have traffic in front of him," said Patrice Bergeron, referring to Price — it's impossible not to come away with the fear that, again, the Bruins have found themselves unprepared for a playoff series.

It's early, of course. The B's easily could tie up the series with a victory tomorrow night. But losing Game 1 means the Bruins must win at least one game at the Bell Centre to move on to the second round, a tall order considering the way they played in their own building last night.

Make it past the second round?

Win the Stanley Cup?

It's like the old days around here — not the old, old, old days when the Bruins won a couple of Stanley Cups, but the recent old days, when the first round was usually the last round.■

CANADIENS 3 / BRUINS 1

EASTERN CONFERENCE QUARTERFINALS   GAME 2   4-16-11

By Steve Conroy

Well, Bruins fans, you very well may have seen your team for the last time in these parts in the 2010-11 season.

For the second straight game, the B's could not avert an early disaster and were chasing the Montreal Canadiens last night at the Garden before ultimately falling, 3-1, to drop down 0-2 in the Eastern Conference quarterfinal series.

The Bruins surrendered two goals in the first 2:20 of the game and, though their push to even the score was better than in the Game 1 loss, they were unable to catch up to Montreal.

The Canadiens scored late in the second period to regain a two-goal lead after the B's had threatened for a tie. In the third, Montreal was able to lock it down and preserve the lead.

Games 3 and 4 will be played at the Bell Centre, where the B's have not won since Feb. 7, 2010.

"Let's be honest here. Our team has not played at all close to the way we know we can," coach Claude Julien said. "You can out-shoot them and you can do a lot of things, but the mistakes that we've made so far are very uncharacteristic for our hockey team. We need to be better than that. And if they're going to score some goals, they have to earn them better than they have. We had to work pretty

Above: Bruins coach Claude Julien and dejected fans at the Garden watch as the team fell into a 2-0 series hole against Montreal.   Christopher Evans | Boston Herald

hard just to get that one goal. I don't think they had to work as hard to get theirs."

All three Canadiens goals came off turnovers committed by Bruins defensemen, a group that looked a bit discombobulated without Zdeno Chara. The captain missed the game due to a bout with dehydration.

The first costly mistake came in the first minute of the game. Johnny Boychuk, Chara's usual partner, sent a pass into the neutral zone that was picked off by James Wisniewski. The Montreal defenseman went on the attack, taking a shot that B's goalie Tim Thomas (23

Above: *Bruins left winger Daniel Paille skates over the 'Stanley Cup Playoffs' logo on the Garden ice before the puck dropped in the Eastern Conference quarterfinal series against Montreal.* Matt Stone | Boston Herald

saves) stopped. But the fat rebound went right to Mike Cammalleri, who finished the scoring play just 43 seconds in for the 1-0 Canadiens lead.

"I saw (Brad Marchand) and tried to give it to him and their guy stepped up and anticipated it and got the puck," Boychuk said.

Things got even better for the visitors less than two minutes later after Bruins defenseman Dennis Seidenberg was called for interference behind Thomas' net. Off the ensuing draw to the right of Thomas, Patrice Bergeron won the faceoff but defenseman Andrew Ference had a hard time locating the puck in the corner. When Ference did find the puck, he threw it softly toward partner Adam

McQuaid, but the pass wasn't close to connecting and Cammalleri pounced on it behind the net. Cammalleri dished the puck out front to Mathieu Darche for the 2-0 lead at 2:20.

"In a penalty-kill situation you're trying to change sides," Ference said. "Their guy did a good job of jumping to the far post and jumping on the play. It's a tough one to give up on the penalty kill."

The B's did battle back in the second period and halved the lead at 7:38 on a pretty goal from Patrice Bergeron, who took a feed from Marchand for a tap-in off the rush. Just seconds later, David Krejci nearly tied it when he had Montreal goalie Carey Price (35 saves) down and out, but the puck slid off his stick.

With 2:39 left in the second, Yannick Weber, a spare defenseman who was playing for Andrei Kostitsyn (foot), delivered the back-breaking goal. Seidenberg sent a pass through the neutral zone that was picked off by Roman Hamrlik, and the Canadiens defenseman dished the puck to Lars Eller on the counterattack. Thomas stopped Eller's shot but left another juicy rebound for Weber, who scored to make it 3-1.

With the next two games to be played in Montreal, the B's are in grave danger of facing a sweep.

"We've got our backs to the wall," Thomas said, "and we'll see how we respond." ▪

Above: Montreal defenseman Hal Gill and goalie Carey Price stuff Bruins left winger Brad Marchand on a wraparound attempt during the third period of Game 2 at the Garden. *Christopher Evans | Boston Herald*

Left: Bruins defenseman Zdeno Chara attempted to skate in Game 2 against Montreal at the Garden but was a late scratch due to dehydration. *Christopher Evans | Boston Herald*

BRUINS 4 / CANADIENS 2

EASTERN CONFERENCE QUARTERFINALS   GAME 3   4-18-11

By Steve Conroy

The Bruins may have a long way to go in this series, but at least they took the first step in their recovery last night.

After losing their first two games of the Eastern Conference quarterfinals at home — and with most of their fans bidding them good riddance as they left town — the B's beat the Montreal Canadiens, 4-2, at the Bell Centre to get back into the best-of-seven series.

Going into the game, the B's felt like they just needed the first goal to play their game and succeed. Well, it turns out they needed the first, second and third goals, because after taking a 3-0 lead they had to hang on in the end after Tim Thomas let the Habs back in the game with two soft goals.

But after Thomas went a long way toward redeeming himself with late saves on Scott Gomez and Andrei Kostitsyn, Chris Kelly salted the game away with an empty-netter with 26 seconds left.

"It's a long series," said Patrice Bergeron, who had two assists and a plus-3. "We've seen it before and we don't want to quit."

Though it was hairy at the end, this was clearly the B's best game of the series. It was also the highlight of the series for their top

Above: *Bruins defenseman Zdeno Chara, the most hated man in Montreal during the playoffs, hears it from fans at the Bell Centre as he takes the ice for Game 3.*
Stuart Cahill | Boston Herald

Above: Bruins forward Brad Marchand (63), center Rich Peverley (center) and forward Mark Recchi celebrate Peverley's goal in a Game 3 win in Montreal. Stuart Cahill | Boston Herald

line of David Krejci, Milan Lucic and Nathan Horton, who were dominant in the offensive zone. Krejci and Horton netted the first two goals.

"We felt good," Krejci said. "We talked to each other before the game and just said, let's go out there and have fun, just like we did all season. That's what happened. We got a couple of goals. We could have gotten a few more, but I'll take two and the win."

The B's got on the board 3:11 into the game when Bergeron set up Krejci.

But before they did that, they had to avert a potential disaster. Just about a minute into the game, Zdeno Chara, playing his first game at the Bell Centre since he hit Max Pacioretty into the center ice stanchion March 8, tried to get on the ice for a change, but the B's were called for too many men on the ice.

They killed that penalty off, though, and three seconds after it was up, Bergeron found Krejci in the slot and the B's had their first lead of the series.

"I thought that PK was huge to give us

momentum that we needed. Killing it, and especially early, showed that it's not going to faze us," said Bergeron.

The B's could have had a three- or four-goal lead after one, but they had to settle for a 2-0 edge. The second goal again came soon after an unsuccessful Montreal power play. Chara fired a shot that missed the net and hit the end boards behind Habs goalie Carey Price. It bounced out to Horton, who from a bad angle managed to lift the puck behind Price and just over the goal line at 14:38.

Another thing the B's had last night that they didn't in the first two games was good fortune. On the third goal, Mark Recchi harassed Price behind the net and the goalie passed it right to Rich Peverley, who only had to shoot it into the net.

"It was just a lucky play," Peverley said. "I think it hit (Recchi's) shin pad and dropped right in front of me."

Kostitsyn got the crowd back into it at 7:03 of the second when he spun Chara and beat Thomas with a seeing-eye backhander between the pads. Then things became really tight when Tomas Plekanec beat Thomas on a bad-angle shot through the 5-hole.

But down the stretch, Thomas stopped Gomez on an excellent chance in tight and robbed Kostitsyn with a great pad save.

And while the climb is still uphill for them, the Bruins showed they weren't going to go too gently into the night.∎

By Stephen Harris

The true quality of a goaltender isn't only demonstrated by the saves he makes, but also by how he responds after letting in bad goals. He can wilt, lose his confidence and let in more.

Or he can battle like hell to stop every other puck that comes his way.

Tim Thomas, not surprisingly, chose the latter, delivering sensational third-period goaltending to hold off the Canadiens, allowing the Bruins to climb back into the series with a 4-2 triumph last night at the Bell Center.

"You're going to get scored on," Thomas said. "It's how you respond to it that's big. The only thing that matters is winning in the end. Certainly that was what I was trying for, to make sure we won that game. So, yeah, I was happy to get the win. The team needed it. I needed it. So it all worked out good."

But not without plenty of anxiety after the B's took a 3-0 lead early in the second period only to see the Canadiens get an Andrei Kostitsyn goal in the second and another early in the third by Tomas Plekanec, which brought the well-silenced crowd very much back into it.

Both goals came on deep-angle shots that snuck through Thomas' 5-hole.

"Those 5-hole goals are ones you never want to give up," Thomas said. "I think someone might have hit Kostitsyn's stick on the first one just as he was shooting, and it made the puck go in a little different place. And then I didn't pick up the puck on Plekanec, the spin-around, until late. They're not pretty goals, but that's hockey."

But on this dramatic and emotional night, the real hockey for Thomas was in the final 15 minutes, when the Canadiens just poured on intense pressure seemingly shift after shift. They put 15 shots on Thomas, who was at his battling, competitive best, doing everything imaginable to keep the puck out.

"It was nerve-racking, but actually it also felt great because we had the lead," said Thomas, who ended up very busy with 34 saves. "You just kept thinking, 'This is going to feel good if we end up on top. It's going to make this 2½-hour bus ride (to Lake Placid, N.Y.) a lot more enjoyable.'"

There were two keys for Thomas: One, his mates staked him to a quick lead. And two, Zdeno Chara was back after missing Game 2.

"The shoe was on the other foot a little bit compared to the first two games," Thomas said. "We scored early, and it makes a big difference. Obviously the team that

Above: Bruins goalie Tim Thomas stops a bid by Montreal right winger Brian Gionta during Game 3 against the Canadiens.
Stuart Cahill | Boston Herald

scores first doesn't always win the game, but overall, percentage-wise, the odds are in your favor. (Chara) makes a huge difference. He's one of the most important, if not the most important player on this team. He's one of, if not the best defenseman in the league. It's harder to play without him.

"Last game we all wanted to step up for him, but we weren't able to get it done. It was nice to see him back. He's just such a big part of our team."

Thomas, after the tremendously important win, kept the emotions low-key.

"You're down 2-0 in the series, and playing in Montreal is not easy," he said. "So it was a gut-check for us, and we got the job done."

After the two 5-holes, it was gut-check time for Thomas, too, and he also got the job done. Now we've got a series.■

BRUINS 5 | CANADIENS 4

EASTERN CONFERENCE QUARTERFINALS   GAME 4   OT   4-21-11

By Steve Conroy

In another epic game that belongs among the best in this storied rivalry, the Bruins overcame three different deficits to beat the Montreal Canadiens, 5-4, in overtime last night at the Bell Centre and even the Eastern Conference quarterfinal at 2-2.

Michael Ryder scored his second goal of the game 1:59 into OT, taking a feed from Chris Kelly and depositing it behind Carey Price.

Though the Ryder winner marked the first lead change of the game, and series, it was a wild night of momentum shifts, unlikely heroes and clutch saves.

"I hope the people feel like they got their money's worth," said a smiling Tim Thomas (34 saves), "because this game took two years off my life."

It was the fourth straight victory for the road team in this series, a trend the B's hope to change tomorrow night at the Garden.

There were so many instances last night when it appeared the Bruins would be coming home with their backs against the wall, down 3-1. But for a team that has had its heart questioned often since blowing a 3-0 series lead to the Flyers last year, they showed plenty of it last night.

The Habs, upset at their own effort in Game

Above: Bruins players swarm right winger Michael Ryder (73) after his game-winning goal in overtime gave the team a 5-4 victory in Game 4 at the Bell Centre.   Stuart Cahill | Boston Herald

3, came out flying and the B's were lucky to go into the first intermission down just 1-0, on a Brent Sopel goal.

But just 2:13 into the second period, Ryder took a feed from defenseman Tomas Kaberle and beat Price over the glove.

Montreal regrouped after that and poured it

Above: Bruins right winger Michael Ryder (73) celebrates his game-winning goal in overtime as Montreal goalie Carey Price and right winger Brian Gionta (21) react with dejection at the Bell Centre. Stuart Cahill | Boston Herald

on, scoring two goals in 55 seconds. They took the lead again after buzzing the Bruins zone with Brian Gionta eventually feeding Mike Cammalleri at 6:52. Then, the Habs broke in 3-on-2 and Tomas Plekanec fed Andrei Kostitsyn to make it 3-1.

With 21,273 Montreal fans trying to blow the roof off the Bell Centre with their lungs and the B's season hanging in the balance, coach Claude Julien called a timeout.

"I just wanted to slow things down to start with," said Julien. "I just told our team to relax and that there's still half the game left to play, and we had to stick to our game plan."

After that timeout, the Habs went 5:52 with-

out a shot on net and, by period's end, the B's tied it again.

Andrew Ference cut the lead in half when he stepped into a loose puck and blasted it past Price at 9:59. The defenseman then appeared to punctuate the goal by flipping the Montreal crowd the bird, though he denied it afterward.

But the B's were certainly a fired up group, and Patrice Bergeron tied the game when he took a feed from Brad Marchand at the top of the crease and popped it home.

It appeared that all the hard work might go for naught when Bergeron was called for an offensive zone hook 32 seconds into the third period. That led to a shortside power-play goal by P.K. Subban and the Habs were up 4-3.

As they had in two victories in Boston, the Canadiens then went into a defensive shell, but this time maybe a little too heavily. With the exception of a Cammalleri breakaway on which Thomas made a huge stop, most of the action was at the other end.

It's a risky game the Habs play and, this time it burnt them. Chris Kelly, who was sent back to Boston Wednesday to have the bones under his right eye examined, found a loose puck in the crease and slide it under Price with 6:18 left in regulation to tie it.

The B's weren't out of the woods yet. With 2:19 left, Dennis Seidenberg interfered with Plekanec and the Habs had a power play. But the Bruins killed it and got the game to overtime.

In the extra session, the B's got a 3-on-1 rush that was close to being offside. But Kelly followed up a missed shot by Rich Peverley and found Ryder all alone out front for the game-winner.

And now, it's a best of three.

"It says a lot (about the team's character)," said Thomas. "We've been able to do that a few times in the regular season, but this is the playoffs and it's a whole new ballgame. It was great to see us able to do that under play-off. And it was fun to be a part of."∎

Right: Bruins goalie Tim Thomas can't stop Montreal right winger Andrei Kostitsyn's shot during Game 4 at the Bell Centre.
Stuart Cahill | Boston Herald

CANADIENS 1 | BRUINS 2

EASTERN CONFERENCE QUARTERFINALS   GAME 5   2-OT   4-23-11

By Steve Conroy

For the second consecutive game, the Bruins and Montreal Canadiens took their battle to overtime.

And for the third straight contest, the B's came out winners.

In a tense, well-played thriller at the Garden that went to double overtime - and looked nothing like the mistake-filled first four games of this Eastern Conference first-round playoff series - Nathan Horton scored at 9:03 of the fifth period to lift the B's to a 2-1 victory and a 3-2 advantage in the best-of-seven set.

The B's can clinch the series with a win in Montreal in Game 6 on Tuesday night. If they can't seal the deal at the Bell Centre, a Game 7 will be played on Wednesday night at the Garden.

On Horton's winner, defenseman Andrew Ference took a short pass from Milan Lucic, moved down to the top of the left circle and snapped a shot on Montreal goalie Carey Price.

Above: Bruins fans wave their black and gold towels as the team takes the ice prior to the start of Game 5 against Montreal at the Garden.   Christopher Evans | Boston Herald

Horton outmuscled Canadiens defenseman Roman Hamrlik at the right side of the crease and popped home the rebound.

"We knew it was going to be a greasy goal and, you know, it sure was," Horton said.

Both B's goalie Tim Thomas (44 saves) and

Above: Bruins right winger Nathan Horton slides the game-winning goal past Montreal goalie Carey Price during double overtime of Game 5 at the Garden. Christopher Evans | Boston Herald

Price (49) were spectacular. Thomas came out the winner in this duel, thanks in great part to an incredible save he made on Brian Gionta on a 2-on-1 in 5:36 of the second OT, sliding across and stopping the shot with his glove.

"That was without a doubt his best game of the series," coach Claude Julien said. "He said the best was yet to come and he backed it up."

While the first four games were characterized by turnovers and questionable goals, this one was as entertaining for the stickler of execution as it was for the casual fan.

And as with all of these marathon type of games, it eventually became a test of stamina and wills. Montreal defenseman P.K. Subban was the minutes leader with 40:38 of ice time, followed by partner Hal Gill (37:39), then B's

blueliners Dennis Seidenberg (38:15) and Zdeno Chara (37:06).

"We stayed with it and we kept competing," Patrice Bergeron said. "We were trying to tell ourselves that we weren't tired, that we were more fit of the two teams. At that point, it's pretty much mental. It's not your bodies, it's your heads. You have to make sure you stay with it and I thought we did a great job of that."

Brad Marchand gave the Bruins a 1-0 lead at 4:33 of the third period. From the post to Price's left, Marchand fed Bergeron out in front for a one-timer. Bergeron's stick broke on a shot attempt, but the puck went right to Marchand for the deposit into the empty net.

Jeff Halpern evened it up with 6:04 left in

Above: Brad Marchand celebrates with teammates Tomas Kaberle and Mark Recchi after breaking a scoreless deadlock with a third-period goal in Game 5 at the Garden.   Christopher Evans | Boston Herald

Right: Nathan Horton celebrates his game-winning goal in double overtime against Montreal with Bruins goalie Tim Thomas after Game 5 at the Garden.   Christopher Evans | Boston Herald

regulation. The Canadiens won a scrum along the left wall in the Bruins zone and got the puck in deep. Defensemen Tomas Kaberle and Adam McQuaid were outworked, and the Canadiens' Lars Eller eventually dished the puck out front to Halpern for the equalizer past Thomas.

Then came the back-and-forth overtime sessions.

The B's went on a power play with 3:48 left in the first overtime after Brent Sopel tripped Bergeron in the clear. After the 5-on-4 was up, Milan Lucic set up David Krejci all alone, but Price refused to be deked and stopped the shot.

Earlier in the first overtime, Montreal's Mike Cammalleri had an open net to shoot at from straight on, but his bid hit both Bergeron and Chara before going wide.

Then, in the second extra session, Thomas robbed Gionta on what looked like a sure goal.

"The save of the game," Chara said.

Horton willed his way into the right place at the right time and everyone went home happy, save for the Canadiens. But even the losing side had to admit it was a great game.

"That's just good hockey," Gill said. 'Both teams are playing hard and unfortunately we didn't get the win.

"But that isn't the end of it."∎

BRUINS 1 | CANADIENS 2

EASTERN CONFERENCE QUARTERFINALS   GAME 6   4-26-11

By Steve Conroy

Well, here we go again. For the fourth time in as many years, the Bruins are facing a Game 7. And they can only hope that tonight's do-or-die match at the Garden goes better than the previous three.

After doing a good job all series of staying out of the penalty box, the B's gave the Canadiens two lengthy two-man advantages in Game 6, and Montreal capitalized. The Canadiens then retreated into the defensive shell that worked for them in Games 1 and 2 and came away with a 2-1 victory at the Bell Centre to force tonight's high-drama Game 7 proceedings.

"We've got to embrace it and enjoy it," Bruins winger Mark Recchi said. "It's a fun time of year and we have to be ready."

Asked how tough the less-than-24-hour turnaround would be, Recchi shrugged it off.

"It's fine," he said. "We're all in great shape and we've played back-to-back all year. It is what it is."

Perhaps it's a good thing that the B's don't have more than a day to stew over the prospect of a Game 7. Three years ago, they lost to the Canadiens in a Game 7 at the Bell Centre, 5-0. Two years ago, they dropped an overtime Game 7 to the Carolina Hurricanes at the Garden. And last year was the crusher, as they coughed up a 3-0 series lead and a 3-0 Game 7 lead at home

Above: A fan yells through the glass at an unfazed Claude Julien as the Bruins prepared to face Montreal in Game 6 at the Bell Centre. Stuart Cahill | Boston Herald

to the Philadelphia Flyers.

We'll see tonight if the Bruins can reverse those fortunes.

"You have to be (confident)," captain Zdeno Chara said. "It's the most important game of the year and you have to be ready for it."

The B's should be kicking themselves after

Above: A dejected Bruins defenseman Zdeno Chara bows his head as he skates off the Bell Centre ice after Montreal's Game 6 victory.
Stuart Cahill | Boston Herald

Game 6. The Canadiens were down two regulars (forward David Desharnais and defenseman James Wisniewski) to injury and, frankly, didn't play all that well. But Montreal took advantage of its opportunities and the B's yet again did nothing with their power plays. Though they quickly nullified two power plays with offensive-zone penalties of their own, the B's went 0-for-4 in 4:35 with the man-advantage and are 0-for-19 for the series.

While goalie Tim Thomas was the hero of Game 5, Canadiens counterpart Carey Price matched him last night. Price made 31 saves, including two beauties in the final 3:30. First, Price made a pad save in tight on Chris Kelly and then, after Kelly took a high-sticking penalty, David Krejci was somehow left all alone in front for a chance that was smothered by the goalie.

"Carey was outstanding," Montreal coach Jacques Martin said. "He's given us a chance to win every night, and that's what you need in the playoffs."

The night began with a quick whistle that

Above: Center David Krejci of the Bruins can't solve Montreal goalie Carey Price during Game 6 at the Bell Centre. Stuart Cahill | Boston Herald

Right: Center David Krejci maneuvers around Montreal defenseman Hal Gill during Game 6 at the Bell Centre. Stuart Cahill | Boston Herald

nullified what should have been an early Montreal goal when Thomas (25 saves) couldn't control a long shot by Scott Gomez, and Brian Gionta hustled to sweep the puck in. The referees immediately waved the goal off because of the whistle.

A number of fans in the Bell Centre crowd threw their white towels down on the ice, causing a delay and garnering an admonishment from the officiating crew that another outburst would result in a Montreal penalty. Considering the egregiousness of the blown call, there was little chance that the visitors would get the game's first power play, and the B's made it easy for the refs.

First, defenseman Adam McQuaid was caught coming off the bench early and the B's were whistled for too many men on the ice at 8:54. Then, off the ensuing faceoff, defenseman Dennis Seidenberg slashed and broke Mike Cammalleri's stick, giving the Canadiens a 5-on-3 for 1:57. Montreal didn't waste the opportunity, as Cammalleri scored on a bullet from the right circle at 10:07 for the 1-0 lead.

Seidenberg tied it up on a 4-on-4 situation 48 seconds into the second period and the B's appeared to be in business, but they soon found themselves down again - and without one of their top-line players.

At 4:37 of the second period, Milan Lucic rammed Jaroslav Spacek from behind into the boards, with the Canadiens defenseman hitting his head against the glass. Spacek went down and stayed down for a while before being led off with a cut (he would later return). Lucic was hit with a boarding major and a game misconduct.

To make matters worse, Patrice Bergeron shot the puck out of the rink soon after the five-minute power play began for Montreal, giving the home team a 5-on-3 for 1:45. Cammalleri fired a shot that Gomez tipped at the top of the crease and Gionta put past Thomas for the 2-1 advantage.

Thanks to Price, the lead held for the Canadiens. And because of it, an elimination game will be played tonight at the Garden. ∎

CANADIENS 3 | BRUINS 4

EASTERN CONFERENCE QUARTERFINALS   GAME 7   OT   4-27-11

By Steve Conroy

This time, in the end, the Bruins didn't flinch.

After coughing up an early two-goal lead and a late one-goal edge, the B's captured their first Game 7 win in four tries last night. Nathan Horton scored his second overtime game-winner of the Eastern Conference quarterfinal series, lifting the B's to a 4-3 game and series victory over the Montreal Canadiens at the Garden.

Horton took a feed from Milan Lucic in the high slot and blasted a slap shot past Carey Price at 5:43 of OT.

Above: Bruins fans wave the flags of players prior to Game 7 against Montreal at the Garden.
Stuart Cahill | Boston Herald

The tension percolating in the crowd of 17,565 was palpable all night, but it only got worse when the game was forced to an extra session.

But when Horton's shot found the back of the net, all that tension was released in one big roar that emanated from the stands and the Bruins bench.

"For us as a group, it was nice to reward our fans with that, because they've been punished enough," said coach Claude Julien with a wide grin.

The B's will now have a return date in the conference semifinals with the Philadelphia Flyers starting Saturday at the Wells Fargo Center (3 p.m.). The Flyers, of course, punished the Bruins and their fans as much as anyone in their history, coming back from a 3-0 series deficit and a 3-0 Game 7 hole last year.

"I'm not going to lie, it's a good opportunity for us to hopefully exorcise some demons," said defenseman Andrew Ference, who had a pair of assists last night. "I don't put too much stock in history. There are new guys on this team, new guys on that team. This is a fresh start for us. But we learned lessons from last

Above: Center Chris Kelly sends a backhanded shot past Montreal goalie Carey Price to give the Bruins a 3-2 lead midway through the third period of Game 7 at the Garden. Matt Stone | Boston Herald

year, no doubt about it."

The B's certainly showed this year they're not the type of team to fold under pressure. After losing the first two games at home, they won Game 3 in Montreal by building a big early lead. Then they evened the series by eradicating three separated deficits before winning their first OT game of the series. Horton scored the double-OT winner in Game 5 and, after the B's dropped a sloppy Game 6 in Montreal, he delivered the game-winner again last night.

"I think we showed a lot of character," said Patrice Bergeron. "We had to put ourselves in a little bubble and not think about the pressure and what people were saying around us. We stayed resilient all game and all series, and found a way."

Like they had against Philly in Game 7 last year, the Bruins got off to a great start, jumping to a 2-0 lead just 5:33 into the game on goals by Johnny Boychuk and Mark Recchi.

But the Habs' special teams got them back into it. First Yannick Weber scored a power-play goal in the first period and then Tomas Plekanec tied it in the second on a shorthanded breakaway.

It stayed 2-2 until midway through the third. After he belted down Montreal defenseman Roman Hamrlik in the neutral zone, Chris Kelly headed to the net as Hamrlik laid on the ice to get a call that never came. Kelly found a fat rebound of a Ference shot and shoveled a backhander over Price at 9:44 of the third.

But with 2:37 left in regulation, Bergeron was called for a high sticking penalty, helped along by a James Wisniewski head jerk. And with 1:57 left in the third, P.K. Subban tied it when he one-timed a slapper past Tim Thomas to sent the game to overtime and gave the crowd a case of the jitters.

The feeling in the B's locker room?

"We were remarkably calm I thought," said

Kelly, who was stoned by Price on a breakaway shortly before Subban's goal. "We never really panicked too much going into overtime. We were a confident group and realized that if we did stay out of the penalty box, we'd be OK."

Still, there were some shaky moments in OT. At one point, a rebound went off Seidenberg's skate and just missed going into the Bruins net.

But after defenseman Adam McQuaid had gone down low, Horton rotated up top, took the Lucic feed and ripped a shot that appeared to deflect off Jeff Halpern and past Price.

"It was pretty special," said Horton. "It doesn't get any better."∎

Right: Bruins defenseman Adam McQuaid (54), defenseman Zdeno Chara (33) and left winger Milan Lucic mob teammate Nathan Horton after his overtime goal beat Montreal in Game 7 at the Garden
Matt Stone | Boston Herald

ROAD TO REDEMPTION

By Steve Buckley

It's been written and said a thousand times, the Bruins blew it big time last year against the Philadelphia Flyers.

The accepted wisdom is that the Bruins squandered the second-round series, in which they led, 3-0, before losing four successive games - that they collapsed, folded, choked, quit, that sort of language.

But that just isn't accurate.

That's not what happened. There's no denying the essential facts: The B's did become only the third NHL team to go up 3-0 in a best-of-seven, then lose. And they are glad to get another crack at the Flyers, as general manager Peter Chiarelli acknowledged yesterday.

"It's fitting that we're playing them," said Chiarelli, who relishes the chance. "Claude (Julien), I think he mentioned to them prior to the game (Wednesday) that there's a chance, one chance, to redeem ourselves."

But the Bruins don't really need redemption. There was no ignominious collapse in the series last year, no weakness of character by the Bruins. Simply put, this was a series in which six of the seven games - the lone exception a very weak, 4-0 no-show Game 5 loss by the Bruins at the Garden - were tossups.

Each of those games could easily have gone either way. It just so happened that the Bruins got the bounces in Games 1, 2 and 3; the Flyers had Lady Luck on their side in Games 5, 6 and 7.

If we were reminded of anything in the Bruins-Canadiens first-round series, it was the fickle nature of this sport, how the tiniest bit of good luck - like when Mike Cammalleri's shot at an open net in overtime of Game 5 happened to tick off Zdeno Chara's skate blade and bounce wide - can be the deciding factor among 60 minutes or more of intense hockey warfare.

That was how close Montreal came to going up 3-2, with Game 6 back at the Bell Centre. Instead, of course, the Bruins won in double-overtime on Nathan Horton's goal.

So it was in last year's Bruins-Flyers matchup. Recall that in Game 4 in Philly, though they were outplayed much of the way, the Bruins got a game-tying goal from Mark Recchi with 31.5 seconds left and Tuukka Rask gone to the bench — and then came close to ending the series in a sweep when Recchi nearly scored early in OT.

All this is a way of saying Bruins players have no reason to feel defensive or fragile about what happened a year ago. No doubt, media and fans alike will cast this rematch as the opportunity for the Bruins to exact revenge, restore their honor and dignity. Nonsense.

It was a good series last year, likely decided when the Bruins lost their leading offensive threat, David Krejci, with a dislocated wrist in Game 4 - and when Philly got Simon Gagne back from a broken toe in the same game.

In a very even series, those two personnel changes made all the difference. If Krejci hadn't been injured, it's a very safe bet the Bruins would have put away the Flyers and gone on the Eastern Conference final. But the "ifs" and "would-haves" don't mean a thing in the playoffs.

Neither does anything that happened 12 months ago - beyond that reality that going through such difficult experience makes players mentally stronger. Between last year's Philly series and this nail-biter against Montreal, the Bruins should be ready for just about anything that comes their way.

"This (matchup against Philly) probably gives you guys more to write about, I'm sure," said team president Cam Neely. "But we don't have the same team as we did last year, and Philly doesn't have the exact same team, either.

"But (last year is) certainly going to be mentioned a lot and talked a lot about. But first and foremost we've got to concern ourselves about how we play that first game."

The Bruins will face a far different style of play from the Flyers than they did with the Canadiens - whose game plan seemed to be draw a penalty, with a dive or otherwise, score a power-play goal and then sit back and hang on.

The Flyers will be a much more difficult foe. They will attack tenaciously from start to finish and with much bigger and tougher forwards than the undersized Habs. It's going to be very interesting to see how beleaguered defenseman Tomas Kaberle,

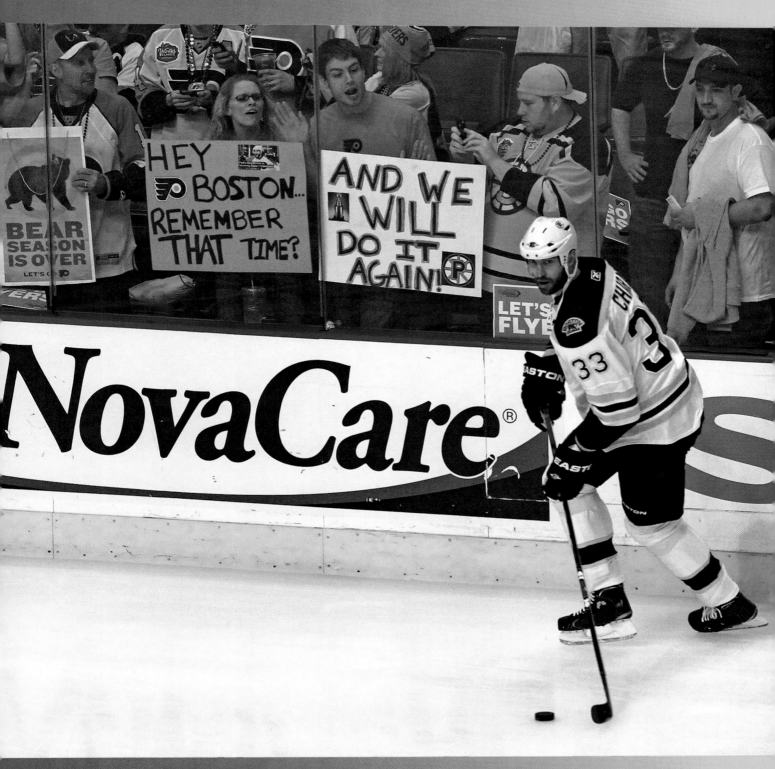

Above: Philadelphia fans remind defenseman Zdeno Chara and other Bruins players of the Flyers' comeback from a 3-0 deficit in the 2010 playoffs.   Stuart Cahill | Boston Herald

who had a poor first series, copes with the Philly forecheckers.

The Flyers are a team the Bruins absolutely can, and probably should beat. They proved in this regular season with a 3-0-1 record — and they proved it in the playoffs a year ago, even if they ran out of luck one game short.■

Bruins left winger Daniel Paille sneaks in on a breakaway during Game 4 at the Garden.

BRUINS 7 | FLYERS 3

EASTERN CONFERENCE SEMIFINALS   GAME 1   4-30-11

By Steve Conroy

With what transpired between these two teams last spring, you may not want to get too excited about the Bruins winning Game 1 of the Eastern Conference semifinals against the Philadelphia Flyers yesterday.

But the road to redemption has to start somewhere, and the Bruins produced about as good a start as anyone that bleeds Black 'n' Gold could have hoped for, crushing the Flyers, 7-3, at the Wells Fargo Center.

"There was so much talk about what happened last year, we wanted to come in and prove that we were ready for the series," said Brad Marchand.

Freed from the shackles of Montreal's suffocating defensive approach, the Bruins' first line dominated. David Krejci had 2-2-4 totals and Nathan Horton added a goal to lead the Bruins. The second line continued its strong play, with Marchand getting a pair of goals, Mark Recchi adding one and Patrice Bergeron notching three assists as the Bruins gave their fans' blood pressure a rare break.

"That was a good game, and you don't usually have those types of leads in the playoffs," said Bruins goalie Tim Thomas (30 saves). "It

Above: Bruins left winger Brad Marchand stuffs the puck past Philadelphia goalie Brian Boucher.
Stuart Cahill | Boston Herald

was nice. But we didn't have that lead the whole game. It was still a playoff game. Philly's known for its comebacks, even within games, so you always have to be on your toes."

The power-play woes continued for the Bruins, as they went 0-for-5, making them 0-

Above: Bruins defenseman Dennis Seidenberg (44) and left winger Milan Lucic (17) congratulate center David Krejci on his goal.
Stuart Cahill | Boston Herald

for-26 in the playoffs. But that was about the only negative in this game, as the penalty-killing unit came up big in crucial spots and the 5-on-5 play was again stellar. One Philly goal came on what was essentially a 5-on-3 in the third period (the first man back on the two-man advantage had just stepped on the ice) and another came on a 4-on-4.

"It's a good start, but it's only one game, right? As we saw last year, they're a team that's not going to quit," said Bergeron, who lived through the historic four-game collapse to the Flyers. "But we're happy with our effort. It was pretty good effort for 60 minutes."

The first line served notice immediately it would be a lot more visible than in the first-round series against Montreal. Krejci put the Bruins up just 1:52 into the game when he took a slap pass from Horton, controlled it and tucked a backhander by Flyers goalie Brian Boucher.

The Flyers got that back when Daniel Briere scored from the top of the crease on a 4-on-4 situation, but Horton gave the Bruins momentum going into the first intermission. Dennis Seidenberg made a pretty move along the right wall, took it down low and sent a pass out to Horton. Boucher stopped the Game 7 hero's first offering, but Horton kept with it and put back his own rebound with 35.7 sec-

Above: Bruins right winger Nathan Horton (18) stuffs the puck past Philadelphia goalie Brian Boucher (33) in the first period of Game 1.
Stuart Cahill | Boston Herald

onds left in the period.

The B's then scored the next three goals in the second period to take a 5-1 lead. First, Recchi had a rebound of his own shot bounce magically back to him and the veteran squeezed the next offering just over Boucher's left pad. Krejci stretched it to a three-goal lead when he tipped an Adam McQuaid shot past Boucher. Finally, Marchand tallied at 17:14, scoring off an Andrew Ference shot that was tipped by Bergeron.

That was it for Boucher. Flyers coach Peter Laviolette sent in Sergei Bobrovsky and, on cue, Philly got the next goal, 16 seconds after

the Marchand tally. Claude Giroux won a face-off in the B's zone over to Sean O'Donnell on the left wall. O'Donnell dished it at the top of the circle to James van Riemsdyk, who beat Thomas with a high shot.

The B's did a good job of keeping the Flyers at bay in the third until a rash of penalties led to Mike Richards' power-play goal with 6:58 left that got them to within two. But Marchand eased things a bit with his second at 14:59 and then Gregory Campbell scored his first playoff goal for good measure.

It was a very good day for the Bruins. ∎

Above: Bruins left winger Brad Marchand (63) holds up his arms after scoring on Philadelphia goalie Sergei Bobrovsky in the third period of Game 1. Stuart Cahill | Boston Herald

BRUINS 3 | FLYERS 2

EASTERN CONFERENCE SEMIFINALS   GAME 2   OT   5-2-11

By Steve Conroy

If you really want to believe in the Bruins, the signs that this just might be their year are starting to accumulate.

The B's took the roundhouse right they were expecting from the Philadelphia Flyers, but they somehow not only shook that off but also withstood a late-game barrage before slipping in their own knockout blow in last night's Game 2 of the Eastern Conference semifinals.

Finishing an absolutely scintillating game, David Krejci took a pass from Nathan Horton and rifled a one-timer over Flyers goalie Brian Boucher at 14:00 of overtime, giving the B's a 3-2 victory at the Wells Fargo Center and a 2-0 lead in the series.

It was the fourth OT win for the B's in nine playoff games, and three of the decisive goals have come from the Krejci line (Horton has scored the other two).

Above: Bruins center Patrice Bergeron (37) and defenseman Andrew Ference (21) congratulate center David Krejci (46) on his overtime goal against Philadelphia in Game 2 at the Wells Fargo Center.   Stuart Cahill | Boston Herald

But the B's would not be in the advantageous position they're in today without Tim Thomas. The 37-year-old netminder picked up his team, which was noticeably sagging in the third period and overtime. He stopped 52 shots in all, including 22 in the third period and 10 in OT.

"You can almost laugh at it. It's unbeliev-

able," said Brad Marchand, one of the three Bruins goalscorers. "It's almost unfair that we have Timmy back there for us. He's made so many great saves. They could have dominated that game, and they did for the most part, but he just made some unbelievable saves."

The night got off to an emotional start. Vocalist Lauren Hart gave her usual rousing

Above: Bruins center David Krejci scores the overtime goal that gives his team the Game 2 win against Philadelphia. Stuart Cahill | Boston Herald

rendition of "God Bless America," which carried added significance following Sunday night's killing of Osama bin Laden.

The "USA! USA!" chants that rang out at Citizens Bank Park a few hundred yards away on Sunday continued at the rink. And it didn't take long for an American to ride the crest of the wave, with James van Riemsdyk, spectacular all night, scoring on a 2-on-1 just 29 seconds into the game. Van Riemsdyk made it 2-0 at 9:31, but the good times in Philly didn't last long.

With their noses bloodied for the first time in the series, the B's came back swinging and tied it up before the period was out, scoring twice in less than two minutes.

They halved the lead at 12:50. Brian Boucher stopped a Tomas Kaberle shot but could not control the rebound. Michael Ryder took a whack at it, but Boucher stopped that one, too. Finally, Chris Kelly swooped in and popped it home for his fourth goal of the playoffs.

Then after Patrice Bergeron prevented a Flyers goal in the defensive zone, he set up the equalizer, dishing the puck out to

Marchand, who tied it on a low wrister at 14:15.

"We knew they were going to come out hard in the first period, and we wanted to weather the storm," Marchand said. "It was great we were able to tie it up there. It looked pretty bad at one point, but we did a good job of coming back and it settled us down."

From there, the night belonged to Thomas. After van Riemsdyk's second goal, he stopped the next 46 shots, including a pad save on van Riemsdyk's bid in the final five seconds of regulation after the B's had just killed off a penalty on Zdeno Chara.

As good as Thomas was, he also was fortunate. The rebound of that van Riemsdyk shot slid out to Danny Briere, who, with a wide-open net, fanned on it just before the horn sounded.

In OT, both teams had their chances, though the Flyers outshot the B's, 10-5. But Philly made the final mistake. Defenseman Braydon Coburn tried a wraparound out of his own zone, but it went right to Horton on the right wing. Horton fed it to Krejci, who blasted the one-timer over Boucher's shoulder and under the crossbar. It was originally waved off and play continued, but the video review clearly showed it was a goal.

Now the B's bring a 2-0 series lead home for Game 3 tomorrow night. They, of course, know no lead is safe against the Flyers, and they themselves proved against Montreal that winning the first two games on the road doesn't guarantee a series win. But 2-0 is better than 1-1.

"It was a matter of will and desire, and somebody had to find a way to win," Bruins coach Claude Julien said. "And that's the one of the things we did well. We found a way to win."

They've been doing that a lot lately.■

Left: Philadelphia goalie Sergei Bobrovsky dives at the puck ahead of left winger Milan Lucic after Bruins center David Krejci hit the post with a shot seconds earlier in Game 2.   Stuart Cahill | Boston Herald

By Steve Conroy

Last week the Bruins exorcised one demon by winning a Game 7 after having their last three seasons ended in the ultimate pressure game.

Now they're on the verge of not only avenging, but obliterating one of the worst memories in franchise history.

For the second straight season, they have taken a commanding 3-0 series lead on Philadelphia in the Eastern Conference semifinals, thanks to a thorough 5-1 drubbing of the Flyers at the Garden last night.

And this year, unlike last, they aim to close the deal, perhaps as early as tomorrow night's Game 4.

"Obviously, the toughest win to get is the fourth win, so we've got to make sure we're ready for (tomorrow)," said center Patrice Bergeron,

Above: Bruins right winger Nathan Horton and Philadelphia defenseman Sean O'Donnell mix it up in the second period of Game 3 at the Garden.   Stuart Cahill | Boston Herald

who played his usual terrific two-way game. "We're happy with tonight's game, but we're going to get right back to work (today) and make sure we work (tomorrow), because Philly's not going to quit. They're a great team and they're going to be there to bounce back (tomorrow).

"So we better make sure we're ready for that."

Zdeno Chara had two goals, an assist and was plus-4, Nathan Horton had a Gordie Howe hat trick (goal, assist, fight), Bergeron had an assist and won an amazing 17-of-19 faceoffs while David Krejci (goal, two assists) scored his second consecutive game-winner and went a perfect 8-0 on draws. Gregory Campbell also had an assist and won 11-of-12 in the faceoff circle.

Tim Thomas stopped 37 shots, but don't let the high shot total fool you. The B's team defense was infinitely better than Game 2 when the Flyers threw 54 shots at Thomas.

Above: Bruins center David Krejci (46) sneaks a shot past Philadelphia goalie Brian Boucher during the first period of Game 3 at the Garden.
Stuart Cahill | Boston Herald

And heck, miracle of miracles, the B's even snapped their 0-for-30 power-play drought with a Chara 5-on-3 goal late in the game.

"I don't know if it was the most complete game (of the playoffs), but it was really one of those solid games in all areas," said coach Claude Julien.

Having been in the position Philly was in last night after they'd lost their first two games at home in the Montreal series, the B's knew what kind of desperate frame of mind the Flyers would be in. But before the visitors could unleash any of that desperation, they found themselves down 2-0 just 63 seconds into the game.

On the opening shift, Brian Boucher made a great save on a Brad Marchand tip-in attempt, but Marchand got the puck back behind the net and dished it out to Chara for a shot Boucher had no chance of stopping just 30 seconds into the game. Thirty-three seconds later, Krejci converted a Milan Lucic pass for a goal.

Flyers coach Peter Laviolette called a time-out to stem the momentum, but it also helped the Bruins stayed focused. And though the B's didn't have a lot of scoring chances the rest of the period, neither did the Flyers.

It stayed 2-0 until 13:39 of the second period, when Daniel Paille scored his first playoff

Above: Bruins goalie Tim Thomas (30) looks skyward as defenseman Dennis Seidenberg salutes him after the team's Game 3 win against Philadelphia at the Garden.   Stuart Cahill | Boston Herald

Right: Bruins left winger Mark Recchi (28) tries to muscle by Philadelphia goalie Brian Boucher in Game 3 at the Garden.   Stuart Cahill | Boston Herald

goal off transition after Johnny Boychuk thwarted what looked like a Flyers scoring chance.

"That was huge," said Marchand. "Going up 3-0 or having it be 2-1 is a big difference. It was kind of a backbreaker for them and it really swings the momentum."

Horton added a 5-hole goal shortly after that and Boucher was pulled for Sergei Bobrovsky. But even though Andrej Meszaros got the Flyers on the board before the second period was out, this one was over.

If the Bruins can keep playing like this, the series will be done by tomorrow night. The Tampa Bay Lightning, who finished a sweep of the Washington Capitals last night, await the winner of this series for the Eastern Conference final. Given what happened to them last year, the B's need to have laser beam eyes on Game 4.

"We are playing it one game at a time, one period at a time, one shift at a time," said Thomas. "We're going to try and play it the same way (tomorrow)."∎

FLYERS 1 | BRUINS 5

EASTERN CONFERENCE SEMIFINALS   GAME 4   5-6-11

By Steve Conroy

The Bruins got their revenge.

A year after blowing a 3-0 series lead to Philadelphia in the Eastern Conference semifinals, they completed the sweep of the Flyers last night with a 5-1 victory at the Garden.

Johnny Boychuk snapped a 1-1 tie at 2:42 of the third period and the B's hung on for the Game 4 win and a date with the Tampa Bay Lightning in the Eastern Conference finals, the first time in 19 years the B's made it that far.

On the game-winner, Chris Kelly won a draw in the left faceoff circle and the puck found its way back to the right point to Boychuk, who blasted a slapper past Sergei Bobrovsky.

Milan Lucic then sealed it with his second goal of the game and of the playoffs with 4:57 left. Nathan Horton stole the puck from Matt Carle at the Philly blue line and sent Lucic on a breakaway. Lucic beat Bobrovsky between the pads.

Brad Marchand and Daniel Paille added empty net goals, and the B's enjoyed a much happier handshake than last year's.

But the news was not all good. Shortly before the goal, the Bruins lost Patrice Bergeron when he took a huge hit from Claude Giroux. He got up slowly, went to the bench slowly and immediately into the locker

Above: Bruins defenseman Zdeno Chara (33) connects with a jab to the head of Philadelphia left winger Scott Hartnell during the first period of Game 4 at the Garden. Stuart Cahill | Boston Herald

room. He did not return. There was no word on his condition.

The Bruins took a 1-0 lead on a first-period power-play goal by Lucic.

But the Flyers tied it at 13:22 of the second. The B's had been buzzing in the Philly end and had several great chances as Paille was stoned by Bobrovsky on a clean break-in. Rich Peverley had Bobrovsky beat, but his backhander went off the side of the net.

Then a 4-on-4 situation was created when Lucic and Scott Hartnell got into a little beef in front of the Bruins bench. Marchand tried to send a turnaround pass along the Flyers

Above: Bruins left winger Milan Lucic celebrates his first-period goal on Philadelphia goalie Sergei Bobrovsky.   Stuart Cahill | Boston Herald

blueline to Dennis Seidenberg, but Mike Richards intercepted, starting essentially a 2-on-0 with Kris Versteeg. Richards dished it to Versteeg, and he made a nice move to his backhand to beat Tim Thomas to the blocker side.

Heading into the clincher, the Bruins had played well in the series, especially in Wednesday's Game 3 win at home, but coach Claude Julien expected the Flyers' best game.

"You're playing a team with some desperation," said Julien a few hours before the game. "Nobody wants to go home and when there's desperation in your game it makes it that much tougher for the team you're closing off. So as I said yesterday, I think it's going to take probably our best effort of the series for us to win this game tonight."

Flyers coach Peter Laviolette decided to go with Bobrovsky after Brian Boucher struggled,

Above: Bruins players salute the Garden crowd after sweeping Philadelphia in the Eastern Conference semifinals. Stuart Cahill | Boston Herald

Above: Bruins left winger Daniel Paille falls as he battles for control of the puck in front of Philadelphia goalie Sergei Bobrovsky and defenseman Matt Carle in Game 4 at the Garden. Stuart Cahill | Boston Herald

especially in Games 1 and 3.

Julien, however, wasn't changing his approach.

"I think every team's prepared for anything right now," said Julien. "When you play the same team in a series, you pre-scout everybody. They do the same thing to us. So, no, it doesn't really matter to us who they put in net. I think we're prepared for whatever scenario is thrown at us. Now it's just a matter of going out there and doing the job and doing it right."

For Laviolette, he was trying to get his team to win one game.

"We didn't try to get to this point just so that we could try to climb out of it again. We certainly wish we were in a different situation, a different scenario, but we are not," said Laviolette. "Our objective is to win one game."

But they didn't.∎

TIM THOMAS

By Stephen Harris

It may not always seem that way as he nightly performs miracles of athleticism in front of the Bruins net, but Tim Thomas is human, and thus subject to the same frailties and uncertainties as anyone else.

And when you're 36 years old in a young man's game, you've lost your job to a 23-year-old rising star the previous season and you've undergone major offseason left hip surgery, you'd better believe that creates uncertainty.

"I did have doubt," said Thomas, who will make his third NHL All-Star Game appearance today. "I mean, of course I had the doubts. I had the doubts, but I was willing to face them and try to prove even the doubts in my own head wrong."

Let's be real here. As this season approached did anyone actually believe that Thomas, who wasn't 100 percent recovered from what was especially major surgery for a goalie, could take the B's No. 1 job back from Tuukka Rask?

Let alone that Thomas would return to form and be the top goaltender in the league - maybe even, as one respected analyst opined last week, the top player at any position?

Even Thomas was hardly sure. What he was sure of, was that he was going to give it his very best shot.

"I was thinking about it all summer," Thomas said. "I told an uncle of mine I was looking at this, in boxing terms, as the biggest fight of my life. That's the way I was going into it all summer - that was training for the biggest fight of my life. I was rehabbing my hip, but also training to be ready.

"I wanted to see how good I could be before it was too late."

The answer: Unbelievably good.

Thomas has delivered his finest NHL season (he feels two years in Finland were comparable) in carrying the inconsistent Bruins to the top of the Northeast Division. He has a 24-5-6 record, a 1.81 goals-against average and a .945 save percentage, plus seven shutouts.

Talk to a few of Thomas' peers during this All-Star weekend, and players who know him well - personally, or as an opponent - aren't entirely surprised by his bounce-back season.

"Timmy is a fighter," former teammate and Toronto Maple Leafs All-Star Phil Kessel said. "He's had to fight his whole career. It is pretty amazing what he's done. Timmy has been fantastic. You watch some of the highlights and I still don't know how he saves some pucks. I've had a couple of chances on him and I just can't score on the guy."

Tampa Bay's Martin St. Louis, a former University of Vermont teammate of Thomas, knew how hungry his longtime friend was to resurrect his career this season.

"I'm not surprised by this," St. Louis said. "Timmy is a battler. He's been a battler his whole career. Last year his numbers were good, they just weren't as good as Tuukka Rask's. As we all know, Timmy needed surgery to fix an injury he had a tough time playing through last year. He still played and did pretty well, but now you can tell, when he's on top of his game physically and mentally, what type of warrior he is.

"I'm proud of him. I'm happy for him. But I'm not surprised."

Still, it was entirely possible that Thomas might never have gotten the chance to do what he's done. Rask, who last year led the NHL in GAA (1.97) and save percentage (.931), figured to be handed the No. 1 job this season. Thomas could have been relegated to the backup post from the start. He knew that could happen.

"The reality is that the goalie that finished up the year playing the majority of the minutes is kind of going to get the first kick at the can the next year," Thomas said. "That's fair. But both guys are going to get a kick at the can.

"I was prepared that Tuukka was going to get a good opportunity. But I also knew that I was going to get some opportunity. I was trying to be ready to take advantage of it when I did get to play."

Thomas admits he was a bit surprised by how quickly he recovered from his May surgery to repair a major tear in the labrum and bone spurs.

"In hindsight, I was closer than I expected to be (at the start of the season)," he said. "Part of that was just what the doctors were telling me after the hip surgery. 'It's going to take a full 3-4 months.' But the way I was feeling by a month after the sur-

Above: Bruins goalie Tim Thomas makes a leg save on Vancouver center Ryan Kesler in Game 6 of the Stanley Cup finals.
Matthew West | Boston Herald

gery, I was already so far ahead of the way I'd felt in such a long time. I was hoping that early on it that would immediately translate to the ice.

"There was still some pain at the beginning of the season, but it only took a couple of weeks before that was gone. And all of a sudden I started to get my movement back. It was like, 'This is fun.'"

St. Louis is well aware of the remarkable career path Thomas has followed — with the seasons in Europe and the minors, and not reaching the NHL until shortly before age 30. With making it big despite an unorthodox style many hockey people derided. And then this comeback, which for St. Louis is just one more chapter in an incredible tale.

"Everybody has their own story," said St. Louis. "Some start later than others, some finish earlier than others. I see Timmy going a long way."

Thomas has heard questions about the possibility of one day making the Hall of Fame.

"I don't even want to think about that," Thomas said. "As far as the Hall of Fame goes, that's still a pipe dream. And if it ever were to happen, it wouldn't be because I spent a lot of time being focused on that. I'm just focusing on the now and trying to play as long as I can."

Besides, he knows very well that goaltenders who don't win Stanley Cups, don't make the Hall of Fame.

"Yeah," Thomas said, "and those are missing from my resume so far."

That's the battle still to be fought.■

Bruins players mob goalie Tim Thomas after polishing off Tampa Bay in Game 7 at the Garden.   Stuart Cahill | Boston Herald

LIGHTNING 5 | BRUINS 2

EASTERN CONFERENCE FINALS   GAME 1   5-14-11

By Steve Conroy

The Bruins played their first Eastern Conference finals game in 19 years. If they want to play their first Stanley Cup finals game in 21 years, the B's will have to be a lot sharper than they were last night at the Garden.

The Tampa Bay Lightning scored three quick goals in the first period and that was more than enough to hold the Bruins at bay, as the visitors took Game 1, 5-2.

Sean Bergenheim, defenseman Brett Clark and Teddy Purcell scored in a span of 85 seconds in the first period and, after Tyler Seguin scored for the B's later in the first, Marc-Andre Bergeron put the game out of reach with a power-play goal at 13:37 of the third. Simon Gagne added an empty-netter for Tampa Bay before defenseman Johnny Boychuk scored a garbage-time goal for the Bruins, but few fans were left in the Garden to see those last two tallies.

The fatal first period wounds were largely self-inflicted.

"The first three goals, I don't think there was a good goal out of all of them," coach Claude Julien said. "Give them credit for their opportunities. That's part of the game. But I think you've got to look at your team and see what you can do better, and we can be better

Above: A young Bruins fan hangs on Bobby Orr's statue prior to Game 1 of the Eastern Conference finals against Tampa Bay at the Garden. Christopher Evans | Boston Herald

at puck management. That wasn't there (last night)."

The B's came out of the gate skating pretty well, but some decent early scoring chances never made it to Tampa Bay goalie Dwayne Roloson (31 saves), as the Lightning skaters did a good job of blocking shots (eight in the first period, 17 overall).

Midway through the opening period, the roof caved in on the Bruins. First defenseman Dennis Seidenberg lost his stick when he was

Above: Bruins center Tyler Seguin scores on Tampa Bay Lightning goalie Dwayne Roloson during the first period of Game 1 at the Garden.
Christopher Evans | Boston Herald

checked by Steve Downie during a blind reverse. A few seconds later, after Tim Thomas could not control a rebound, Seidenberg could only kick at the loose puck, which went right to Bergenheim for his NHL-leading eighth playoff goal at 11:15.

Just 19 seconds later, the Lightning had a 2-0 lead on a softie. Clark went coast-to-coast and beat Thomas between his the right arm and his body on a backhander.

"Backhanders are always a little harder to tell where they're going to go," Thomas said. "I was looking for who he was going to pass it to, then I was trying to figure out who he was...for tendencies. Then he went backhand and backhanders are always hard to tell where they're going to go. I was just trying to put my chest in the center of the net and it was just a seeing puck."

If the Clark score wasn't bad enough, the third goal was a killer. Seidenberg sent a soft pass to defense partner Tomas Kaberle behind the net, but Kaberle couldn't handle it. Purcell grabbed the loose puck at the side of the net

Above: Bruins left winger Brad Marchand attempts a wraparound shot on Tampa Bay goalie Dwayne Roloson during the second period of Game 1 at the Garden. Christopher Evans | Boston Herald

and jammed it in short-side at 12:40.

"The puck slid off my blade when I tried to make a move," Kaberle said. "Those things you have to put behind you."

Seguin, in the lineup in place of Patrice Bergeron (concussion), brought the B's back to within two goals later in the first period on a terrific move and shot past Roloson.

But the loss of Bergeron was felt throughout the night. The B's won just 39 percent of their faceoffs — David Krejci was beaten on 15-of-18 draws — and lost far too many of the other battles throughout the night.

"It's so important to start with the puck," Julien said. "When you don't win as many draws as you're used to, you're backpedaling a bit and we know how quickly they counter. It certainly didn't help our game."

The Bruins did have chances to get back into the game, but the power play let them down again (0-for-4). The B's also fired 16 shots that missed the net.

"Execution and killer instinct are some things that need to be better on the power play moving forward here," Julien said.

Overall for the B's, a lot has to be better.■

Above: Bruins left winger Milan Lucic and Tampa Bay right winger Adam Hall vie for the puck during the third period of Game 1 at the Garden.
Christopher Evans | Boston Herald

LIGHTNING 5 | BRUINS 6

EASTERN CONFERENCE FINALS   GAME 2   5-17-11

By Steve Conroy

Firewagon hockey is usually not the Bruins' blueprint for success. But then again, the entire toolbox of Tyler Seguin had yet to work on the template. Until last night.

In a wild, up-and-down game featuring a coming-of-age performance by the 19-year-old rookie, Seguin spearheaded a five-goal second period with two goals and two assists (on linemate Michael Ryder's goals) to lead the Bruins to a 6-5 win at the Garden in Game 2 of the Eastern Conference finals.

The Bruins took a 6-3 lead into the third period but then had to hang on for dear life - thanks to a Grant Fuhr-like performance by Tim Thomas (36 saves, 13 in the third period) - to even the best-of-seven series at 1.

"It's about as uncharacteristic as it's going to get for us," Mark Recchi said with a relieved laugh.

Coach Claude Julien acknowledged the things that went well - the spectacular effort by Seguin, improvement on faceoffs (56 percent) and the domination at times in the Lightning zone - and he wasn't going to quibble too much about a playoff win. But he certainly didn't like the way his team finished it off.

"Just because we won the game doesn't mean we're happy with it," Julien said. "We got

Above: Bruins left winger Mark Recchi puts a massive hit on Tampa Bay defenseman Mattias Ohlund in the second period of Game 2 at the Garden. Matthew West | Boston Herald

sloppy."

But that explosive second period was enough to give them a win. While it wasn't a perfect game for the B's, they did show some heart. The Lightning's Adam Hall scored 13 seconds into the game and, after Nathan Horton tied it with a power-play goal, Martin St. Louis gave Tampa Bay the lead back with 6.5 seconds left in the period after the B's had pretty much set up shop in the Lightning zone.

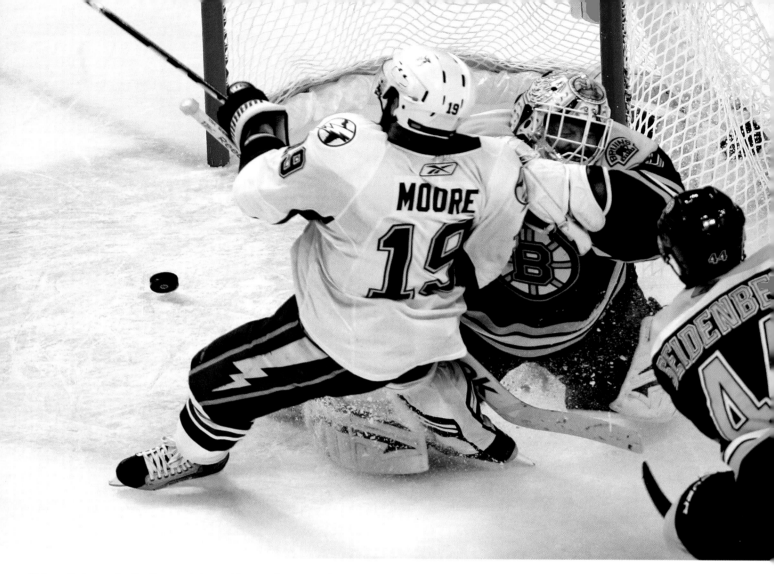

Above: Bruins goalie Tim Thomas takes out Tampa Bay center Dominic Moore while making a second-period save in Game 2 at the Garden.
Matthew West | Boston Herald

That St. Louis goal could have been a killer, but it had the reverse effect on the B's.

Seguin tied the game 48 seconds into the second period when he scored on a break-away. Ryder sprung Seguin and, after the rookie twisted Randy Jones into a pretzel, he took a major league hack from Victor Hedman. But Seguin kept going and beat Dwayne Roloson with his patented backhand move.

Then the B's took their first lead of the series at 2:24 as they dominated in the Lightning zone. Horton sent a high pass to Dennis Seidenberg, sliding down from the right point. Seidenberg sent a beautiful pass down to David Krejci for a tap-in goal from the top of the crease.

The B's took a 4-2 lead at 6:30 on Seguin's third goal in two games. Adam McQuaid pushed a puck ahead out of the B's zone to create a 2-on-1 for Horton and Seguin. Horton dished it over to the hot hand and Seguin roofed the puck over Roloson. Seguin's skills were pretty evident at this point, but the veteran Recchi was impressed by something else.

"The biggest thing for me is he's competing. When he's competing like that, things fall into place for him," Recchi said.

The Lightning fought back and, after Recchi took a cross-checking call in front of the B's net, Vincent Lecavalier drew the Bolts back to within one with a power-play goal at 7:48.

But the B's kept on the pressure, and Seguin continued to be a major factor. He saw his

Above: A shot by Bruins right winger Michael Ryder is denied by Tampa Bay goalie Dwayne Roloson during Game 2 at the Garden.
Matthew West | Boston Herald

Right: Bruins forwards Tyler Seguin and Michael Ryder celebrate Ryder's second-period goal as fans at the Garden erupt in the background during Game 2.   Matthew West | Boston Herald

first power-play time of the postseason after a Lecavalier penalty and promptly helped produce a goal. Roloson could not handle his sizzling slap shot and Ryder was there to lift the rebound home at 16:16. Ryder tucked another backhander by Roloson with 19 seconds left in the period and it seemed like the rout was on.

Not so. Coach Guy Boucher lifted Roloson for Mike Smith, who saw eight very easy shots in the third. Meanwhile, Tampa Bay poured it on at the other end. Steven Stamkos made it

6-4 at 3:47 off a Zdeno Chara turnover in the neutral zone and at 13:15, Dominic Moore made it a one-goal game.

But that's as close as the Lightning would get, though they threatened until the final 15 seconds of the game.

"There's going to be adversity in the playoffs," said Chris Kelly. "I think things like that make you stronger in the long run. We'll try to correct those mistakes and move forward."

At least they can move forward with a win.■

BRUINS 2 | LIGHTNING 0

EASTERN CONFERENCE FINALS   GAME 3   5-19-11

By Steve Conroy

Well, now that's a little more like it.

Game 3 of the Eastern Conference finals didn't have nearly the entertainment value of Game 2, but no one in the Bruins' traveling party was complaining, least of all coach Claude Julien.

Last night, the B's got back to their sound defensive system, notched a couple of timely goals and let Tim Thomas see just about every one of the 31 shots he faced as the Bruins silenced the 21,027 gathered at the St. Pete Times Forum with a 2-0 victory over the Tampa Bay Lightning.

The B's took a 2-1 series lead with Game 4 tomorrow afternoon.

"I think (last night's) game probably resembled a lot more of what everyone expected from this series," said Julien. "Two teams that can make it hard for you to score and I thought our team was very good in regards to that. We made some stronger plays, some better decisions and we seemed a little bit more aware out there of what was going on.

"So comparing it to last game, where I thought it was pretty sloppy, I thought we bounced back well."

The players were just as pleased.

"We played a more compact game, we played a smarter game," said winger Milan

Above: Bruins goalie Tim Thomas blocks a close-range shot by Tampa Bay right winger Martin St. Louis during Game 3 action at the St. Pete Times Forum. Stuart Cahill | Boston Herald

Lucic, who had one of his best games of the playoffs. "It showed in Game 1 and Game 2 that when we opened up and played run-and-gun, it's probably not the best thing for us. Everyone loves a 6-5 game, but as a coach and as a player, you get a heart attack when you see that chance-for-chance.

"But I think we did a good job playing as a five-man unit. We can enjoy that win (last night), but definitely there's a lot more work to be done."

Above: Bruins right winger Nathan Horton collides with Tampa Bay left winger Simon Gagne along the boards at the St. Pete Times Forum during Game 3. Stuart Cahill | Boston Herald

Lucic helped get it started when he fed David Krejci in front for the first goal just 1:09 into the first period. He beat Tampa Bay defenseman Brett Clark in the right corner after Johnny Boychuk kept it in. Nathan Horton was open for an instant in the high slot, but the Lightning rushed to collapse on him. That left Krejci all alone at the top of the crease.

Lucic zipped it over to Krejci, who held the puck for what seemed an eternity, then went to a backhand move that spun Lightning goalie Dwayne Roloson to the ice. He flipped it into the empty net.

"It's a great way to get the game started," said Lucic. "That first goal is huge."

Having scored first for the first time in the series, the Bruins then got more confident. With Patrice Bergeron (18-for-28 in faceoffs) back in the lineup for the first time since suffering a concussion on May 6, they also seemed a lot calmer. They were not turning it over in the neutral zone, nor allowing a whole lot of odd-man rushes.

One of the few Tampa Bay did get was as dangerous as they come, as Martin St. Louis and Vincent Lecavalier broke out on a 2-on-1 in a first period 4-on-4 situation, but defenseman Zdeno Chara made a great play to break up the St. Louis pass.

Chara and the rest of the defense played extremely well throughout the night. And it was fitting that a defenseman provided the insurance goal at 8:12 of the third period. Andrew Ference collected a feed from Michael Ryder and one-timed a slap shot that somehow made it through a few bodies and barely trickled through Roloson's pads.

"Shots go off shin pads or it hits one of their guys and it sits there for a rebound," said Ference. "It's nice to get blocks, but they cause goals, too. Throw enough at the net and you can get lucky."

But that's about the only thing that was lucky for the Bruins in this victory.

Make no mistake, they earned this one.∎

Right: Bruins players congratulate center David Krejci (46) on his first-period goal during Game 3 at St. Pete Times Forum.
Stuart Cahill | Boston Herald

BRUINS 3 | LIGHTNING 5

EASTERN CONFERENCE FINALS   GAME 4   5-21-11

By Steve Conroy

Throughout their current playoff run, the Bruins had done a terrific job of living the cliches of taking one period at a time and keeping their eyes on the task at hand.

Then came yesterday.

The B's took a 3-0 first-period lead only to see the Tampa Bay Lightning score three goals on four shots in a span of 3:48 in the second. Then Simon Gagne scored what turned out to be the game-winner at 6:54 of the third. Martin St. Louis added an empty-netter and the Lightning had themselves a 5-3 victory in Game 4 of the Eastern Conference finals.

So instead of returning home with a 3-1 series lead with a chance to close it out in Game 5 at the Garden tomorrow night, the Bruins are in a 2-2 series that is now a best-of-three.

"I think we might have taken (a win) for granted," Brad Marchand said, "and it bit us in the butt."

The B's staked themselves to the three-goal lead by continuing the good works from Game 3.

Patrice Bergeron scored the first of his two unassisted goals when he capitalized on a bad exchange between Tampa Bay defensemen Victor Hedman and Brett Clark and popped the gift puck past Dwayne Roloson. Michael

Above: Bruins left winger Milan Lucic (17) and center David Krejci (46) tangle with Tampa Bay defenseman Eric Brewer behind the Lightning goal during Game 4 at the St. Pete Times Forum.
Stuart Cahill | Boston Herald

Ryder made it 2-0 when he scored on a 2-on-1, before Bergeron scored what should have been a backbreaking shorthanded goal, stealing the puck from Steve Stamkos in the neutral zone and scoring on a long-range shot that went between Roloson's pads.

Bergeron's second goal ended Roloson's afternoon, as Lightning coach Guy Boucher inserted backup goalie Mike Smith.

Whether the change sparked Tampa Bay or not, it was a completely different team in the

Above: Tampa Bay left winger Sean Bergenheim beats Bruins goalie Tim Thomas 5-hole as defenseman Adam McQuaid looks on during Game 4 at the St. Pete Times Forum. Stuart Cahill | Boston Herald

second period. For the first time since the series shifted venues from the Garden to the St. Pete Times Forum, the Lightning started to win battles. And it was a puck battle that got Tampa Bay going.

After a little miscommunication between goalie Tim Thomas and Zdeno Chara on an exchange behind the net, Ryan Malone caved in the flat-footed defenseman and the puck squirted to Gagne, who sent it out front. Teddy Purcell collected the puck, curled into the slot and beat Thomas with a backhander at 6:55.

"I guess (Thomas) kind of got caught between passing it or handling it himself," Chara said. "Then he just ran out of options. There were too many people and very little time."

A minute and three seconds later, Purcell zipped his second goal under the crossbar. Then it was all tied up after Sean Bergenheim relieved Tomas Kaberle of the puck behind the net, stepped out front and scored - and it was a brand new hockey game.

Coach Claude Julien thought his team lost focus after taking the lead.

"The message was pretty clear: We had to continue playing the same way. But somehow we started getting stretched out again. They started getting speed. They started getting momentum," Julien said. "And after they scored a few goals, we almost looked like we were paralyzed out there. We just weren't reacting, weren't moving, and it just snow-

Above: Bruins left winger Brad Marchand levels Tampa Bay center Steven Stamkos (91) during Game 4 at St. Pete Times Forum.
Stuart Cahill | Boston Herald

Above: Dejected Bruins players skate off the St. Pete Times Forum ice after squandering a 3-0 lead in a Game 4 loss to Tampa Bay. Stuart Cahill | Boston Herald

Below: Bruins coach Claude Julien gestures to the referee during Game 4 at the St. Pete Times Forum. Stuart Cahill | Boston Herald

balled from there."

The second period ended with the teams tied at 3, and the B's had entered the game 5-0 in the playoffs when tied after 40 minutes. That perfect record went out the window with the Gagne goal in the third period.

Malone picked off an errant Milan Lucic pass in the neutral zone and moved in on Thomas. The puck was shoveled forward by Malone and went off Dennis Seidenberg's stick. Gagne, who scored the game-winner for the Flyers after the B's lost a three-goal lead in Game 7 of the Eastern Conference semifinals last year, wound up with the puck and slipped it between Thomas' pads.

The B's did have a few chances to tie. Smith's best save came with 1:50 left when Nathan Horton tipped defenseman Andrew Ference's shot. The deflection appeared labeled for the shortside, but Smith was able to pin the puck between his right pad and the post.

St. Louis iced the game on his empty-netter with 37 seconds left.

Now the B's must deal with whatever kind of hangover a collapse like that can have.

"We have to forget about this one as quick as possible," Seidenberg said. "There's no reason for us to dwell on this game too long. In the past we've turned the page pretty quickly, and I don't see any reason why we can't do that again."■

LIGHTNING 1 | BRUINS 3

EASTERN CONFERENCE FINALS   GAME 5   5-23-11

By Steve Conroy

The Tampa Bay Lightning had their chances to blow out the Bruins in Game 5 of the Eastern Conference finals last night at the Garden.

They didn't capitalize on their chances, and the Bruins made them pay.

After the Lightning took the first lead of the game just 1:09 in and outshot the B's, 14-4, in the first period, Nathan Horton and Brad Marchand scored second-period goals for an improbable lead. The Bruins played some great lock-down defense (with the help of goalie Tim Thomas) in the third period, and Rich Peverley added an empty-netter with 12.1 seconds remaining for a 3-1 win.

Up 3-2 in the series, the B's are one win away from their first Stanley Cup finals appearance since the 1989-90 season. They can close out the Lightning tomorrow night in Tampa.

"It wasn't our best game," coach Claude Julien said. "But sometimes it's about finding ways to win."

Last night, the B's leaned on some of the organization's cornerstones - Thomas, Zdeno Chara, and Patrice Bergeron - to secure the win.

Thomas made 33 saves, one that might have been the stop of the entire playoffs. Chara (plus-2, assist) was a beast at both ends, forcing the issue on the game-winning goal and helping frustrate the Lightning in the

Above: Bruins center Rich Peverley celebrates after sealing the team's Game 5 win against Tampa Bay with an empty-net goal at the Garden. Matthew West | Boston Herald

defensive zone. Bergeron (plus-2, assist) had his usual heavy-on-the-puck presence and made a brilliant pass to Marchand on what turned out to be the game-winning goal.

And after the Bruins blew a 3-0 lead in Game 4, it's the Lightning's turn to lament what might have been.

Above: Bruins goalie Tim Thomas makes the save of the series, a lunging stop with his stick during the third period of Game 5 at the Garden.
Matthew West | Boston Herald

After Simon Gagne scored on a 2-on-1 early in the first, Tampa Bay had the Bruins reeling. The Bolts dominated the first period, and at one point kept the puck in the offensive zone on a power play for the entire two minutes. But in the end, the Lightning's vaunted man advantage was 0-for-4, and because of that, they're heading back home on the verge of extinction.

"It was one of those games where you dig deep and find a way to win," Milan Lucic said. "Obviously, Timmy after giving up an early goal, he kept us in it and made some great saves. It's the playoffs. No matter how you get 'em, we're obviously happy to get a win."

Horton was trying hard to put the goat horns on his head. He took an interference penalty at the end of the first period and then another one early in the second. But on his first shift after the B's killed his second penal-ty, the first line made a nice play off a faceoff to get the B's even. David Krejci, much better on the dot (14-of-22 in faceoffs) than in Game 4, won a draw in the right circle and Lucic, stationed at the inside of the circle, pounced on it. Lucic took the puck to the halfboards then curled off and sent a perfect backhand pass to Horton, who rifled a shot past goalie Mike Smith at 4:24.

While the B's (outshot 34-20 in the game) weren't peppering Smith with shots or pres-sure, they slowly were wrestling away control of the game from the Lightning. And they got the go-ahead tally at 15:56, with Chara leading the charge. At the offensive blue line, the defenseman chipped the puck in then fol-lowed it up, gaining control on the right side before Bergeron took over. Bergeron zipped a pass across the top of the crease to Marchand, who redirected the puck past Smith.

"I decided to carry it on my own and put a little soft chip on and go after it," Chara said. "It made them turn it over, and from that point we had some guys that had position on their guys, and then Bergy obviously made a nice play. Marchand was driving to the net and got rewarded."

In the third, Thomas made a couple of great saves. First, he got a piece of a Blair Jones shot that rang the post. Midway through the period, he absolutely robbed Steve Downie after Eric Brewer sent a shot just wide that bounced off the endboards. Downie had an open net, but Thomas lunged back and made a stick save that will be replayed many times in the next few days and beyond.

"That was a game-saver," Chris Kelly said. "It was unbelievable."

The B's played extremely well defensively down the stretch, and when Peverley buried the empty-netter, they finally were able to breathe easy. Until tomorrow night.

Asked what they needed to do to close out the series, Chara didn't mince his words.

"Play better than we did (last night)," the captain said.■

Left: Bruins defenseman Andrew Ference sends Tampa Bay center Steven Stamkos into the net with a cross check during Game 5 at the Garden.
Mattew West | Boston Herald

BRUINS 4 | LIGHTNING 5

EASTERN CONFERENCE FINALS　　GAME 6　　5-25-11

By Steve Conroy

The Bruins have been thumbing their noses at conventional wisdom throughout their playoff run.

By tomorrow night, conventional wisdom just might get them in the end.

They have improbably made it to the third round of the postseason with barely the trace of a power play. But the Tampa Bay Lightning last night forced a Game 7 in the Eastern Conference finals thanks largely to the continued failure of the Bruins power play and the sudden re-emergence of their own.

The Lightning cashed in on three of their four power plays while the Bruins went 1-for-5. As a result, the Bolts walked out of the St. Pete Times Forum with a 5-4 win. The series will conclude at the Garden tomorrow night.

The B's got an excellent game from their first line,

Above: Bruins left winger Brad Marchand and Tampa Bay right winger Steve Downie vie for the puck during Game 6 at the St. Pete Times Forum.　Stuart Cahill | Boston Herald

with David Krejci notching a hat trick and Milan Lucic getting a goal and an assist. And the Bruins did scrap back in the third period after twice falling behind by two goals. But they didn't get enough pucks at a less-than-stellar Dwayne Roloson (16 saves) and, despite dominating down the stretch territorially, they finally succumbed.

Now they must win another Game 7 at home, as they did against Montreal in the first round. And the Bolts have to win another

Game 7 on the road, which they did in Pittsburgh in the opening round.

"Nobody said it's going to be easy. Nobody said it's going to be a series with one team dominating," captain Zdeno Chara said. "It's an even series with one game to go. The winner moves on and the loser goes home."

Though the B's did score on their fifth man-advantage, the numbers are not pretty. The Bruins are now 5-for-61 on the power play - and remember, they had the Lightning down

Above: Bruins defenseman Andrew Ference cross checks Tampa Bay center Steven Stamkos during Game 6 at St. Pete Times Forum.
Stuart Cahill | Boston Herald

3-0 in Game 5 and had two power plays early in the second period which they squandered.

The Lightning, of course, came back to win that game and even the series at 2-2. Had the B's converted on one of those two chances in that game, they might already be making their travel plans to Vancouver for the Stanley Cup finals.

Instead, they're facing a do-or-die game.

"Throughout this playoff, other than the first two games of the first series, we've been able to bounce back (from a loss), but it's going to be our toughest challenge," said

Lucic, who was a strong presence in the offensive zone all night. "We need to put together a full 60 minutes. Once again in this building for some reason, we didn't have a good 60 minutes.... We've got to find a way to play a full 60 minutes."

After Teddy Purcell scored his first of two goals just 36 seconds into the game, the B's took a 2-1 lead into the second on goals from Lucic and Krejci.

But the Bolts regained the lead in the second period on goals from Martin St. Louis and Purcell with Dennis Seidenberg and Rich

Above: Bruins goalie Tim Thomas makes the stop on Tampa Bay center Vincent Lecavalier during the second period of Game 6 at St. Pete Times Forum.   Stuart Cahill | Boston Herald

Peverley in the box, respectively. They took a 4-2 lead on another power-play goal from Steven Stamkos, with Andrew Ference in the box, just 34 seconds into the third.

The Bolts would need that pad goal, and more. For the B's finally cashed in on a power play at 9:46 when, with Chara working down low, Krejci was left open to redirect a Nathan Horton feed to make it 4-3.

But just 29 seconds later, the Bolts scored what would be the winning goal. Johnny Boychuk, on the ice for seven of the nine goals scored, pinched down from the right point but didn't get the puck, and Tampa Bay took off on a 2-on-1. Steve Downie fed St. Louis, who beat Tim Thomas (21 saves).

The B's fought back again, as Krejci was somehow able to sneak a puck under Roloson for his third goal of the game at 13:28. But that's as close as they would get. They pushed

Above: Bruins defenseman Dennis Seidenberg levels Tampa Bay right winger Martin St. Louis during Game 6 at the St. Pete Times Forum.
Stuart Cahill | Boston Herald

till the end but, after pulling Thomas with 1:28 left, they couldn't extend the game.

Now they must win this series on home ice that they earned.

"You play 82 games and a lot of people say, what do you play 82 games for?" said coach Claude Julien. "That's one of the key things, that if you can get home-ice advantage for this time of year, you need to take advantage of it.

"We did against Montreal and now we need to do the same thing against Tampa."∎

LIGHTNING 0 | BRUINS 1

By Steve Conroy

The Bruins played close to a perfect game in Game 7 of the Eastern Conference finals last night at the Garden. And it was just barely enough.

On a night when Tampa Bay Lightning goalie Dwayne Roloson was on top of his game, the Bruins scored the lone goal of the incredibly intense contest at 12:27 of the third period and advanced to their first Stanley Cup finals in 21 years with a 1-0 victory.

While the B's didn't get the goal until late in the game, they seized control of the contest from the get-go with terrific all-around play. With the 17,565 fans whooping it up from well before the puck dropped, the Bruins never disappointed them in this one, and now they have a date with the Canucks, starting with Game 1 on Wednesday in Vancouver.

"They were our seventh man tonight," veteran Mark Recchi said of the fans. "We felt it and we could hear it inside the dressing room.

Above: A decorated Bruins fan gets ready to cheer on the team prior to Game 7 against Tampa Bay at the Garden. Christopher Evans | Boston Herald

We could hear the excitement, the chants. It was incredible. A great feeling. Guys were like, 'They're ready. Let's go out and get this.'"

That they did.

Nathan Horton, who had overtime winners in Games 5 and 7 of the first round against the Montreal Canadiens and missed the sec-

Above: Bruins center David Krejci controls the puck in front of Tampa Bay center Steven Stamkos during Game 7 at the Garden.
Christopher Evans | Boston Herald

ond half of the first period last night after taking a big hit, redirected a perfect pass from David Krejci, who took a breakout feed from Andrew Ference.

The defenseman moved the puck deliberately out of his own zone and hit the speeding Krejci with a pass just over the red line, puncturing the Lightning's 1-3-1 defensive system. Krejci gained the offensive zone, crisscrossed with Horton on the left side and then sent the pass back to Horton at the top of the crease

for the tap-in.

It was one of several strong offensive plays by the B's, but the only one that worked. Roloson stopped 37-of-38 shots.

"Obviously their forecheck and their system has been talked about a lot and it is hard to break down. But there are cracks in it," said Ference. "And that's a play that we specifically drew up, specifically talked about throughout the series that was an option, that was available. We must have dumped the puck in 90 percent of the time. But in the back of our heads, we were always looking for that play and the timing worked out perfect. Krejci came through and was available for the pass instead of another dump-in. It just worked."

From there, the B's relied on Tim Thomas (24 saves), Zdeno Chara, Dennis Seidenberg and the rest of the team's dogged dedication to how they want to play hockey. With 7:33 left, they were now focused on keeping the puck out of their own net. But unlike in past games, the B's never looked panicked and never buckled.

"Our mindset was pretty much clear on how we wanted to play and how we wanted to execute. And we never really changed it," Chara said of the 60-minute effort. "Even after the second when it was still 0-0. We knew we had to stick with it and play our way. Eventually, you need just the one play. And that's what happened."

Now the Bruins will play the best team in the NHL in the Canucks. They will be underdogs, for sure. But for this night, it was hard to quibble with what the B's accomplished.

"It's something that this team, this organization, this city has been waiting for for a long time," said Chara. "So obviously, we are very excited. We can enjoy the moment but we are going to go back to work (today)."

Actually, they'll go back to work tomorrow, as coach Claude Julien gave his players the day off today. They earned it.■

Right: Bruins right winger Nathan Horton scores the series-clinching goal against Tampa Bay during Game 7 at the Garden.   Stuart Cahill | Boston Herald

COACH CLAUDE JULIEN

By Stephen Buckley

We might not be having this discussion had the Bruins been whacked by the Montreal Canadiens in the first round of the Stanley Cup playoffs.

That's because Claude Julien probably would have been escorted from his office out to Causeway Street by TD Garden security officers, and then, two days later, yet another newly minted coach would be smiling into the television cameras and promising a New Deal for long-suffering Bruins fans.

But the Bruins held off the Habs in Round 1, and then swept the Flyers in Round 2.

And here we are, in Round 3, with the Bruins needing two more victories over the Tampa Bay Lightning in the Eastern Conference finals to advance to the Stanley Cup finals. Game 4 will be played this afternoon at the St. Pete Times Forum, with the Bruins holding a 2-1 lead in the best-of-seven series.

For Julien, it's a chance to be the coach of a Stanley Cup-winning team. But it also means job security: With the Bruins having made it this far into the spring, hasn't he earned the right to remain head coach for next season and possibly beyond?

True, the Bruins could go belly up against the Lightning, and then, well, you never know.

As of now, though, Julien has helped make Boston sports history: For the first time, the coach/managers of all four of the Hub's big league sports franchises have been on the job for at least four consecutive seasons.

Bill Belichick, the dean of Boston's coaches, took over the Patriots in 2000. Terry Francona has been managing the Red Sox since 2004. Doc Rivers was named coach of the Celtics for the 2004-05 season. And Julien has been coaching the Bruins since 2007-08.

And it turns out this is not just a coincidence. While Julien has yet to coach his team to a championship, as Belichick, Francona and Rivers have done, his incumbency is in some ways tied to the longevity of his three coaching peers.

Speaking with the Herald yesterday, Julien, recalling the new deal he received last year from general manager Peter Chiarelli, said, "When Peter met with me and we agreed on a contract extension, one of the things he said is that he'd like to get some stability here, like the other organizations in Boston have had.

"And to me that means a lot," Julien said. "As a coach, it's a tough job and the one thing you want to do is work in an area where you get to know the people and get to know the city, and make that city your adopted city.

"I'm happy that I've been able to be here four years, and I'm hoping to be here longer."

It hasn't always been easy. Boston being Boston, Julien has received no small amount of criticism. He heard it two years ago, when the Bruins were eliminated in the second round by the Carolina Hurricanes. He heard it last year, when they blew a 3-0 series lead to the Flyers in the Eastern Conference semifinals. And he is hearing it even now, with some B's fans wondering why it took the coach so long to get wunderkind Tyler Seguin into the line-up.

"I heard about it from other people," Julien said. "I don't really pay attention to that. It didn't bother me, because we don't take this job to be popular. We take this job because we enjoy doing what we do, and we know that criticism is part of that.

"Sometimes you hear things that really don't make any sense," he said. "But from the inside you know what's really going on ... I've blocked off everything on the out-

Above: Bruins coach Claude Julien yells at his team after calling a timeout against Tampa Bay during the first period of Game 1 of the Eastern Conference finals.   *Christopher Evans | Boston Herald*

side. You're never going to kill me with that kind of stuff."

Does this mean Julien knew his job was safe even if the Bruins had gone out in one of the earlier rounds?

"Who am I to say, right?" he replied, the suggestion being that that his job may well have been in jeopardy had the Bruins gone down in the first or second round. "All I know is that right now we have a good group of guys here who believe in what we're doing. We don't have to twist their arms.

"They're believers," he said. "They seem to enjoy the process, and I haven't seen any resistance at all. And I haven't felt any resistance." ▪

By Steve Conroy

The Bruins usually owned the third period this year, as they did 5-on-5 play.

But the Vancouver Canucks took control of both in Game 1 of the Stanley Cup finals last night and, with the time running out in regulation, they finally threw a puck at the net that Tim Thomas had no chance of stopping and handed the B's an excruciating 1-0 loss at Rogers Arena.

Raffi Torres scored with just 19 seconds left to lift the Canucks to victory on a play that was started by Ryan Kesler.

Johnny Boychuk came out to play the puck just in front of the Bruins' defensive blue line near the left boards, but Kesler tipped the puck behind him and just barely kept his toe picked into the blue line to keep the play onside.

Above: A Bruins fan runs into a Vancouver fan outside Rogers Arena prior to the start of Game 1.
Christopher Evans | Boston Herald

Once along the left half wall, Kesler found Jannik Hansen near the right circle. All of a sudden, Hansen had a 2-on-1 with Torres and Zdeno Chara as the only Bruin back. Chara went to the ice to block the cross pass to Torres, but Hansen got it through and Torres one-timed it past Thomas.

"It was a long pass up (from Kevin Bieksa) and I tried to step up and stop the pass," Boychuk said. "I don't know where it went

after that, but (Kesler) got it, he passed it over and I don't know if it was a 2-on-1 or a 2-on-2, but I was trying to get back and I couldn't."

Thomas made 33 saves and was 19 seconds away from posting his sixth consecutive shutout period. Still, he was tremendous. The Canucks came out flying on their first several shifts and Thomas had to make several high-quality saves immediately. And he was terrific in the third period, stopping Maxim Lapierre

Above: Bruins left winger Milan Lucic gets flipped on a cross check by Vancouver defenseman Dan Hamhuis during Game 1 at Rogers Arena.
Stuart Cahill | Boston Herald

twice on redirects and then Hansen on a breakaway.

But there was little Thomas could do on the Torres shot.

"He's going to compete, he's going to battle, he's going to do whatever he can to give us a chance to win," Milan Lucic said. "We need to reward him for his efforts and that's the bottom line."

Counterpart Roberto Luongo, meanwhile, did not have to be quite as flashy as Thomas,

but he was awfully good in stopping all 36 shots the Bruins threw at him.

"Yeah, he was good," said David Krejci, who had five shots on net. "I don't think we had a lot of good scoring chances. We had a good one on 5-on-3 when we hit the post, but he made a couple of good saves. We had lots of shots, we have to make sure we get traffic in front of him so he can't see the shots."

Both teams had chances to take the lead prior to that, but both went 0-for-6 on the

Above: Bruins center Patrice Bergeron is taunted by one of the Green Men as he sits in the penalty box during Game 1 at Rogers Arena.
Christopher Evans | Boston Herald

power play. The B's also crapped out on a 5-on-3 that lasted 1:32 at the start of the second period. Mark Recchi had the best chance to score but his shot off a cross pass hit the outside of the post.

As the game wore on, the Canucks got the better of the scoring chances. They threw 14 pucks at Thomas in the third period, with the last one finally beating him.

"I thought for the first two periods we played a pretty even game," said B's coach Claude Julien. "Obviously, in the third we just seemed to lack some energy and lost our legs. They just seemed to come at us pretty hard. They kind of took the game over in the third period and obviously found a way to win it with a late goal."

It was a pretty nasty game, highlighted by a scrum at the end of the first period when

Patrice Bergeron got in a shoving match with Alex Burrows and apparently got his finger bitten by the Canucks forward.

Burrows could at least get a talking to from the NHL brass and possibly a suspension, though he was given only a double-minor for roughing in the game.

This series could really start to percolate.

"We haven't played this team all that much. We've only played them three times in the last three seasons, so you want to create that hate right off the start," said Lucic.

And Lucic sounds like he's building a pretty good chip on his shoulder.

"All you guys are doubting us, so we showed (last night) that we can play with them," he said. "We worked hard, we played but, especially in this building, we're going to have to play a little harder." ∎

Above: Bruins center Patrice Bergeron and Vancouver left winger Alex Burrows mix it up during Game 1 at Rogers Arena.

Christopher Evans | Boston Herald

BRUINS 2 | CANUCKS 3

STANLEY CUP FINALS   GAME 2   OT   6-4-11

By Steve Conroy

Two games into the Stanley Cup finals, the Bruins have had their hearts broken twice.

After Raffi Torres scored the game-winning goal with 18.5 seconds left in Game 1, an Alex Burrows goal ended Game 2 last night just 11 seconds into overtime, giving the Vancouver Canucks a 3-2 victory and a 2-0 series lead.

While the second dagger certainly had to leave a wound on the B's, they insisted it wasn't mortal as the series shifts to the Garden for Games 3 and 4.

"We've come back from two down and we had to go on the road (against Montreal). We're going home," said Mark Recchi, who scored one of the two Bruins goals. "We're going to be disappointed and we have a right to be. But (this) morning when we step on that plane, it's forgotten about. We'll focus on Game 3. And we're going home to our crowd, and it's pretty exciting there as well."

But it certainly seems like the magic is running out. It was the first time in five tries that the B's did not prevail in overtime in this post-season.

On the game-winner, Patrice Bergeron won the center ice faceoff back to Andrew Ference and the defenseman tried to bank the puck

Above: Bruins defenseman Zdeno Chara collides with Vancouver left winger Jeff Tambellini during the first period of Game 2 at Rogers Arena.   Stuart Cahill | Boston Herald

Right: Vancouver right winger Maxim Lapierre, left, vies for the puck with Bruins right winger Nathan Horton during Game 2 at Rogers Arena.   Stuart Cahill | Boston Herald

off the boards in the neutral zone to Recchi. But the puck went beyond Recchi to Canucks defenseman Alex Edler, who immediately turned it back up ice to Daniel Sedin. From there, Sedin dished the puck up to Burrows, who broke in on both Zdeno Chara, rushing over to defend, and goalie Tim Thomas.

Coming out aggressively to cut down the

angle, Thomas forced Burrows behind the net, but the goalie spun out on the fresh ice and Chara was a step behind Burrows. The Canucks forward was able to beat the defenseman and tuck the puck into the net on a wraparound.

It was a tough end to a night on which the Bruins again hung with the Canucks without playing a great game. In the first period, the visitors had a terrible time handling the puck. In the third, the B's lost a one-goal lead when the Canucks for the second straight game were the better team in a period that they have usually owned.

"It's our own fault," coach Claude Julien said. "We beat ourselves with some bad decision-making and poor puck management. You take responsibility and you make the corrections that you have to. And you move on."

Burrows, who escaped suspension from the league after biting Bergeron's finger in Game 1, had a monster night, scoring two goals and assisting on Sedin's equalizer at 9:37 of the third period. Julien flatly rejected the opportunity to carp about the fact that Burrows was on the ice while some may have felt he should have been suspended.

"If we use that as an excuse, then we're a lame team," Julien said.

It was a tough night for Chara. The captain was on the ice for both B's goals and picked up an assist on Recchi's power-play tally, but he was also on for two of the Canucks' goals and was in the penalty box for the first one. Ference also had giveaways on the first and third Vancouver goals.

The Canucks got on the board in the first period on the power play after Ference's clearing attempt was stopped. Burrows eventually beat Thomas to the shortside.

The B's had their best period of the series in the second, when Milan Lucic beat Roberto Luongo and Recchi tipped a Chara wrister past the Vancouver goalie 2:35 later for their first lead of the series.

But in the third period, the Canucks again took over and tied the game. In overtime, it didn't take long for disaster to strike.

"We didn't come here just to roll over," Julien said. "We're going to go home, regroup and bounce back." ■

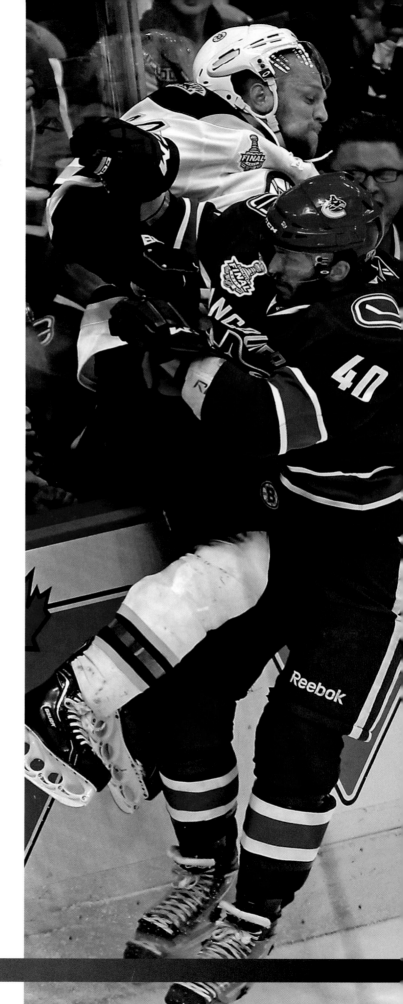

Left: Vancouver right winger Maxim Lapierre checks Bruins defenseman Dennis Seidenberg into the boards during Game 2 at Rogers Arena.
Stuart Cahill | Boston Herald

Above: Bruins left winger Milan Lucic celebrates his goal as Vancouver goalie Roberto Luongo (1) lays on the ice and defenseman Christian Ehrhoff looks on in shock during Game 2 at Rogers Arena.   Stuart Cahill | Boston Herald

CANUCKS 1 | BRUINS 8

STANLEY CUP FINALS   GAME 3   6-6-11

By Steve Conroy

You might have been hard-pressed to find a hockey expert who thought the Bruins were a more skilled team than Vancouver before these Stanley Cup finals began. But hockey is also a game of emotion and, boy, did the Canucks ever stir those emotions in the B's during Game 3 last night at the Garden.

After Canucks defenseman Aaron Rome knocked Nathan Horton out of the game with a blatant, scary shot to the head early in the first period, a shaken B's team finally got off the mat and buried the Canucks with a second period full of figurative haymakers before landing a couple of literal ones in the third.

The B's won, 8-1, and climbed back to within a game of the Canucks, who have a 2-1 series lead. Mark Recchi scored two goals, Michael Ryder posted 1-2-3 totals, and five other Bruins had multiple-point nights.

Tim Thomas, meanwhile, returned to his excellent form to get the win, making 40 stops, many spectacular. And in a must-win situation, the B's left no doubt.

"There have been tests throughout the year and also in the playoffs for this team, to focus and to show up," said defenseman Andrew Ference, who opened a four-goal second peri-

Above: A Bruins fan holds a replica Stanley Cup outside the Garden prior to Game 3.
Christopher Evans | Boston Herald

od with his third tally of the playoffs. "It wasn't a perfect game. There were still turnovers, there were still mistakes, bad penalties. You still had some of those things. But we had a little more focus and a little more grit. ... It wasn't pretty. It was Boston hockey."

The game, the first Cup finals contest in Boston in 21 years, started festively enough. Shawn Thornton was in the lineup for the first time in this series, and he decked new villain

Above: Johnny Boychuk of the Bruins congratulates teammate Daniel Paille after Paille scored a third-period goal during Game 3 at the Garden. Christopher Evans | Boston Herald

Alex Burrows, who bit Patrice Bergeron in Game 1, on his first shift. The B's were well into their process of establishing a tone when Rome apparently tried to do something about that.

Horton carried the puck through the neutral zone and dished it to Milan Lucic on his left. He had taken about four strides when Rome stepped up on the blue line and delivered a very late hit to the head. On top of the hit he absorbed, Horton's head bounced off the ice

and his arm shot straight in the air like a boxer who's been knocked out. It appeared to be a textbook violation of Rule 48, regarding blind-side hits to the head, that was enacted last year after Matt Cooke's hit on Marc Savard.

"It was a blind-side hit that we've talked about taking out of the game," Bruins coach Claude Julien said.

A hushed crowd watched Horton loaded onto a stretcher, and he was taken to Mass.

Above: Bruins defenseman Zdeno Chara rearranges Vancouver right winger Maxim Lapierre's face shield during the first period of Game 3 at the Garden.   Matthew West | Boston Herald

General Hospital. It was reported that he was moving all his extremities, but there was no further news.

Rome received a game misconduct and the B's got a five-minute power play out of it, but at that point they were still a little stunned to do much with it. But they would gear it up soon enough.

"We were obviously very worried about him. He's obviously a key guy on our team and he's family to us," center Brad Marchand said. "To see him in that position was tough to see and tough to take. But we regrouped after that first period and came out hard."

Did they ever. Ference scored 11 seconds into the period, Recchi made it 2-0 on a power play, Marchand netted a highlight-reel short-handed goal, and David Krejci scored off a fat rebound given up by Roberto Luongo.

With the outcome all but established, referees Dan O'Rourke and Stephen Walkom kept a steady parade of players going to the penalty box and the dressing rooms in the third, but the B's added four more goals, from Daniel Paille (another shorthanded tally), Recchi, Chris Kelly and Michael Ryder (another power-play goal). Meanwhile, 10-minute misconducts were dished out to Vancouver's Daniel Sedin, Burrows, Ryan Kesler and Kevin Bieksa, and the Bruins' Ference (twice), Lucic, Thornton and Dennis Seidenberg in a 98-penalty minute third.

Above: Bruins right winger Nathan Horton lays on the ice after absorbing a vicious hit from Vancouver defenseman Aaron Rome during Game 3 at the Garden.   Christopher Evans | Boston Herald

Considering all the nasty incidents already in the first three games, Ference was asked if he thought if the series was teetering on the verge of getting out of control. He gave a sly smile.

"That's our sport," he said. "I hope it's teetering. That's usually pretty good hockey, as long as it doesn't cross over too much. That's what people pay to come watch."

And whether the B's win another game in this series or not, they proved they're a team you toy with at your own peril.■

CANUCKS 0 | BRUINS 4

STANLEY CUP FINALS   GAME 4   6-8-11

By Steve Conroy

We have ourselves a brand new Stanley Cup finals.

In Game 4 of this utterly enthralling best-of-seven tilt, the Bruins again dominated the Vancouver Canucks last night in a 4-0 victory at the Garden to even the series, with Game 5 to be played tomorrow night back at Rogers Arena.

The Canucks cannot get back home fast enough. In the two games at the Garden, Vancouver was outscored 12-1, saw its vaunted power play (0-for-4 last night, 1-for-22 in the series) disintegrate and had its prized goaltender Roberto Luongo blown up.

The B's got two goals from Rich Peverley and one apiece from Michael Ryder and Brad Marchand, while Tim Thomas (38 saves) stood tall in the shutout, with a lot of help from his entire six-pack of defensemen.

There will be one more game at the Garden this season and the Bruins will either be looking to clinch the Stanley Cup or fighting for their lives. But the B's have to love the way they protected their home ice.

"The way we played, we came from the drop of the puck and we didn't let up for most of the night," Shawn Thornton said. "They played hard, too. We had some pucks go in and

Above: A Bruins fan and Vancouver fan mix it up in front of the Bobby Orr statue prior to Game 4 at the Garden. Matt Stone | Boston Herald

Timmy stood on his head. It's going to be a great series. We tied it up and now we are going to have to work on the next one."

The B's 8-1 beatdown of the Canucks in Game 3 was packed with emotion, but this victory did not take a back seat to the previous one in that regard. The night began when none other than Bobby Orr was introduced as the honorary captain, which revved the fans up enough. But when Orr was handed a giant

Above: Bruins defenseman Dennis Seidenberg takes Vancouver left winger Alex Burrows down to the ice as goalie Tim Thomas looks to join the melee during Game 4 at the Garden. Matt Stone | Boston Herald

flag with Nathan Horton's name and number on it, the roof was all but ripped off the building.

As far as orchestrated moments go, it was as goosebump-inducing as they come, perhaps topped only by a brief appearance in the locker room by Horton himself after the game. And the B's seized the moment by the throat.

The Canucks again would flash their skill at times in the first period, but as was the case in both home games for the Bruins, there was little substance behind it. And when Peverley, taking over the concussed Horton's spot on the first line, beat Luongo through the 5-hole on a breakaway at 11:59 of the first, the B's again had the upper hand. The Bruins would go on to score twice in the second period and once in the third, but in reality they only needed the one.

As the game wore on, either the Canucks' vaunted speed wasn't what it was made out to be or they just quit, because the B's were getting to all the loose pucks.

"I thought that as a whole team, we played really tight defensively and we made some strong plays," captain Zdeno Chara said. "And that's what you need, obviously, to have everybody contributing."

Ryder gave the B's some breathing room at 11:11 of the second when his wrister from the top of the circle, which was deflected by Canuck defenseman Sami Salo, slipped under Luongo's arm.

And then the B's simply outworked the Canucks to take a 3-0 lead at 13:29. Marchand knocked a puck away from Keith Ballard and may have gotten away with a trip. Henrik Sedin was there to support his defenseman, but Patrice Bergeron swiped the puck away from Sedin and got it out from to Marchand, who shoveled it past Luongo's glove.

Peverley added his second goal at 3:39 of the third when a Milan Lucic feed went off his body. The fourth goal was the 12th allowed by Luongo over five-plus periods, and Vancouver coach Alain Vigneault decided to replace his star netminder with local product Cory Schneider.

Do the B's think Luongo got rattled?

"Our job is to get pucks and bodies in front of him," Dennis Seidenberg said. "Whether we rattled him or not, it doesn't really matter. As long as the pucks go in."

And if they keep going in at this rate, this dream of a Stanley Cup will become a reality.∎

Right: Bruins left winger Milan Lucic eyes the puck after eluding Vancouver center Henrik Sedin during Game 4 at the Garden. Stuart Cahill | Boston Herald

BRUINS 0 | CANUCKS 1

STANLEY CUP FINALS   GAME 5   6-10-11

By Steve Conroy

The Stanley Cup will be in the house when the Bruins play their final home game at the Garden on Monday night, but they won't want to see it just yet.

The Bruins got pushed to the brink of elimination last night in a 1-0 loss to the Vancouver Canucks at Rogers Arena, giving the Canucks a 3-2 series lead in the Cup finals despite the fact that the Presidents' Trophy winners have scored a grand total of six goals in five games.

The B's must win Monday to force a Game 7 back here Wednesday. And a one-game, winner-take-all situation would seem to be a fitting ending for this series. But they have to take care of business in Game 6 first.

"We've just got to give ourselves a chance to get back here," captain Zdeno Chara said. "Now it's all about Game 6. I've said it before: You can't get too high or too low, and we have to turn the page."

Last night was an opportunity for the B's to wrestle away control of this series, and they didn't play badly. But in the end, they just didn't get enough pucks and bodies at Canucks goalie Roberto Luongo, who had given up 12 goals in the previous two games but last night stopped all 31 shots he

Above: Bruins right winger Shawn Thornton and Vancouver right winger Maxim Lapierre exchange words during Game 5 at Rogers Arena.   Christopher Evans | Boston Herald

Right: Bruins defenseman Dennis Seidenberg hangs his head as he skates past cheering Vancouver fans after the Canucks took a 1-0 lead in Game 5 at Rogers Arena.
Christopher Evans | Boston Herald

saw. And he did see just about all of them.

"A good effort. Not good enough," said coach Claude Julien. "At times when we should have gotten the puck in deep and establish the forecheck, we turned pucks over. And give credit to (Luongo). He certainly played well. But we certainly didn't make it as hard on him as we did in the last two games."

Maxim Lapierre scored at 4:35 of the third period, breaking Tim Thomas' shutout streak at 110 minutes and 42 seconds. Seconds after being robbed by Thomas (24 saves), Lapierre scored when Kevin Bieksa shot the puck wide from the right point and it bounced off the end boards right to Lapierre on the left side.

Thomas got a piece of the shot, but he couldn't keep it from falling over the

line for the only goal of the game. The Canucks were able to protect that slim lead for their third one-goal victory in this series, all at home.

This game was tantalizingly there for the Bruins to take, especially in the

early going when the B's got three first-period power plays. But the B's could do nothing with them and would go 0-for-4 with the man-advantage on the night.

"Tonight was certainly not a good night for a power play. It wasn't a good night for our whole team, as far as creating good, quality scoring chances," Julien said. "We had some, but the thing, again, that we need to do a lot better is get to that front of the net. We had guys there, but on the side. We need to be a little more aggressive in that area than we were tonight. That's so huge for our hockey club and we need that."

After being embarrassed in two games at the Garden, the Canucks certainly looked like a team that had its collective manhood questioned. They came out trying to hit everything in a white jersey and, though it got them in penalty trouble early on, it set a tone. The Canucks were credited with a whopping 47 hits while the B's only had 27.

"They were pumped up and played with a lot of energy in front of their home crowd," Chara said.

And on Monday, the B's need to feed off the energy of their own crowd like they did in Games 3 and 4.

"I don't think we're a team that's done anything the easy way, so in certain ways, it's not surprising that we're here in this situation where we've got to bring our team back home and create a Game 7," Julien said. "Two of the last three rounds we have been through seven-game series, so our goal right now is to create another one." ∎

Above: Bruins defenseman Adam McQuaid, right, falls to the ice after tangling with Vancouver center Ryan Kesler during the first period of Game 5 at Rogers Arena.   Christopher Evans | Boston Herald

By Steve Conroy

The Bruins have not played one game to win the Stanley Cup since that night in Madison Square Garden 39 years ago when Bobby Orr triumphantly picked up the puck and jumped into Gerry Cheevers' arms, champions once again.

There has been a lot of heartbreak since then, but the 2010-11 Bruins - not given much of a chance to beat the Canucks when these Cup finals began - earned their way into a winner-take-all Game 7 tomorrow night in Vancouver.

Facing elimination, the B's exploded for four goals in 4:14 in the first period, and then ground out a comfortable 5-2 victory in Game 6 last night.

"The last time I talked to you guys I said it was do-or-die for us, and we approached it that way," captain Zdeno Chara said. "We were pretty sharp and we played the game of our lives."

Whether the Bruins come home with the Cup, they at least saved three of their best, most emotional performances for their home fans in this series. Now they've got to find a way to bottle at least a portion of that home potion and bring it to Vancouver, where they have scored only two goals over three games.

It will be the first Cup finals Game 7 in Bruins history.

"It's the last game of the season and this is what you play for," said defenseman Johnny Boychuk, who picked up an assist. "We've done a good job in elimination games and hopefully we can bring that into Vancouver."

Indeed, the B's are 3-0 in elimination games this postseason, but all three have been on home ice. And as was the case after Game 4, they appear to have rattled Roberto Luongo as

Above: A Bruins fan holds up a sign taunting the Canucks prior to Game 6 at the Garden.   Matthew West | Boston Herald

Above: Bruins right winger Michael Ryder extends for the puck between Vancouver left winger Raffi Torres and defenseman Andrew Alberts during Game 6 at the Garden. Matthew West | Boston Herald

the teams head back across the continent. The Canucks goalie was yanked after just 8:35, having given up two softies and another goal on a screen, something that's been missing dearly from the B's game in Vancouver.

Brad Marchand got things going at 5:31. Mark Recchi poked a puck through Christian Ehrhoff in the neutral zone and Marchand gathered it up at the blue line. He went down to the outside right circle and snapped off a wrister that somehow beat Luongo high to the short side.

At that point, all the scorn of the Bruins fans came raining down on Luongo, who had given an ill-timed critique of Tim Thomas' style after Game 5. And Luongo didn't handle it well. Just 35 seconds later, Milan Lucic sift-

ed another soft goal through Luongo's pads and the howls grew even louder.

Finally, after Andrew Ference used a Recchi screen to fire a power-play goal by him at 8:35, coach Alain Vigneault yanked Luongo for Cory Schneider. But just 1:10 later, Michael Ryder tipped home a Tomas Kaberle shot and the B's could start revving the engines of their charter plane to take them to British Columbia.

Though the game was in the bag, the Canucks, it should be noted, did not tuck tail this time when they were down, forcing Thomas (36 saves) to make some excellent stops late in the first and beating him with a couple of goals in the third from Henrik Sedin early and Maxim Lapierre late. (David Krejci

Bruins left winger Milan Lucic celebrates
a first-period goal with teammates as
fans at the 'Garden erupt in the back-
ground during Game 6.
Matthew West | Boston Herald

would also add a 5-on-3 goal for the B's.)

The Canucks will likely be ready tomorrow night. And the B's have to be better than they were in the three previous games in Vancouver.

"I think we are very well aware of how we've played on the road the last three games in Vancouver," coach Claude Julien said. "It hasn't been good enough and our plan is certainly to change that for Game 7. We've created ourselves another opportunity and it's up to us to take advantage of it. But we've got to be hungrier than we have been the last three times in Vancouver and want to put some pucks at the net and get ourselves hungry around that net area."

And if the B's bring that requisite hunger, then who knows?

Maybe this wild playoff run just might have one ecstatic ending.■

Above: Bruins left winger Brad Marchand celebrates his first-period goal with Patrice Bergeron and Mark Recchi as Vancouver center Henrik Sedin skates off in Game 6 at the Garden.
Matthew West | Boston Herald

Left: Right winger Michael Ryder celebrates the Bruins' fourth goal in the first period of Game 6 at the Garden.   Matthew West | Boston Herald

BRAD MARCHAND

By Ron Borges

Brad Marchand calls himself "a rat," but he's our rat and so, to us, he's just a pest. And no place loves its pests more than Boston.

That's the beauty of being a scrappy, little guy in a town like this. Blue collar down to our underwear, Bostonians look at the highly skilled Sedin brothers and laugh when Mike Milbury calls them "Thelma and Louise" because of their less-than-stout approach to the hammer side of hockey. Bostonians look at Marchand and say, "Our kind of guy, Bradley is."

Wednesday night, Marchand exhibited all that the Bruins have long been about, the things that separate this team and this town from Vancouver — the laid-back home of the Canucks. Vancouver fans love the flashy pass and quick shot of the Sedins. Bruins fans love to see them flipped upside down.

Marchand is from the upside-down school of hockey and so a cult hero grows every time he does things like slam his 5-foot-8, 183-pound body into Vancouver's star center, Ryan Kesler, sending him crashing into the end boards, as Marchand did on the first shift of Wednesday night's 4-0 win over the Canucks - a shellacking that sent the Stanley Cup finals back to Canada tied, 2-2.

Vancouver roared into the Hub after two heartbreaking, one-goal Bruins losses, thinking they had control of the Cup. Actually what they had was a ticket to Hockey Hell Night, an 8-1 mental and physical Game 3 beatdown that started only after the Canucks suddenly thought they were the Bruins. Memo to them: You aren't.

Aaron Rome took out Nathan Horton with a cheap shot, knocking him into a fog so deep you felt the Hound of the Baskervilles would soon be trotting onto the ice. Instead out trotted guys like Marchand, and ever since the hard guys with the spoked B's woke up and realized their game is not the Canucks' game it's been 12-1, Bruins.

Their game is Marchand's game. Their game is hard charging, forechecking and hardly a thought of any style but the kind that made Joe Frazier heavyweight champion.

Even after Game 4 was decided, Marchand was still fighting, taking a triple minor on a play in which he violated just about every rule in the NHL's book (roughing, holding and tripping). It was the kind of play that separates Bruins from Canucks.

Marchand roughed up Christian Ehrhoff along the boards with only 2:27 to play and the B's leading, 4-0, and was immediately called for a penalty while the puck was still loose. Marchand went after it and Daniel Sedin tried to run him into the end boards. The NHL "Code" says along the end boards you don't duck an oncoming hit, you take it like a man so the other guy doesn't decapitate himself.

Marchand took another route. He dipped low and sent Sedin flying over his back and upside down on the ice. The Bruins Code? Code Red.

"I tried to jump over Ehrhoff there and clipped him with my arm and a Sedin tried to take a run at me, and that would have been a cheap hit because I already had a penalty against me," Marchand said. "So I just ducked on him and saw (Keith) Ballard come and he had his gloves off so I dropped mine.

"I shouldn't have taken that penalty then, but it's tough riding that line. Obviously it's part of my game to be a bit of a rat out there."

Not many guys admit to such a role, yet Marchand is more than what he seems. He is not a rat. Max Lapierre is a rat. Marchand? He's a pest with pop.

"First of all, he's always been an energy player, a good skater," coach Claude Julien said of Marchand. "Unfortunately, he's been looked upon here in this league more as a pest, stirring things up. What people don't know about Brad is he's got really good skills. He's got a great release, good shot, good speed. He's very capable of playing a good game. Sometimes that gets overshadowed in certain games where he lets the other part of his game take over.

"Whenever he's really focused on his game ... those kind of things start coming out. You see how good a player he can be. He's a much better player than people see him as because some things overshadow his ability to play the game at a high level."

Those things are the kind of check he put on Kesler and the takedown of Ehrhoff, but that constantly pushing, poking, pestering style is also what led to his goal Wednesday night.

Above: Bruins left winger Brad Marchand shoots the puck past Vancouver defenseman Aaron Rome during the first period of Game 1 of the Stanley Cup finals.   Christopher Evans | Boston Herald

It happened not simply because he was in the right spot when teammate Patrice Bergeron outfought Henrik Sedin for a loose puck behind the net and pushed it through to Marchand, who then beat Roberto Luongo to his glove side. It happened because Marchand was forechecking, taking down Ballard behind the net to first knock the puck free. After he did Marchand wheeled around to the front of the net as Bergeron poked the loose puck out front.

Goal, Pest!

"I'm just trying to play my game and what happens happens," Marchand said. "You take pride in whatever aspect of the game you want to play."

Brad Marchand wants to play the aspect that makes the Sedin Sisters stay awake at night. He wants to play hockey Boston style.∎

BRUINS 4 | CANUCKS 0

STANLEY CUP FINALS   GAME 7   6-15-11

By Steve Conroy

The long wait is blissfully over.

After 39 years of heartbreak, mediocrity and, at times, indifference from their once-rabid fan base, the Bruins are Stanley Cup champions and princes of the city once again.

Patrice Bergeron and Brad Marchand both scored twice as the B's defeated the heavily favored Vancouver Canucks, 4-0, in Game 7 of the Cup finals at Rogers Arena last night. Once expected to be run over by the best offense in the NHL, the B's held the Canucks to just eight goals in seven games en route to their first title since Bobby Orr graced the Black 'n' Gold.

And well before the diehard Canucks fans had filed out of the arena and started burning cars, there was little doubt as to which team was the best in the National Hockey League.

"Best feeling in the world, man. Best feeling in the world," said forward Shawn Thornton of his second title, the first one coming with the 2007 Anaheim Ducks.

Tim Thomas was his usual airtight self in the victory that was the pinnacle of the 37-year-old's incredible journey. He made 37 saves to notch his second shutout of the series and was the only logical choice for the Conn Smythe Trophy.

Above: Bruins defenseman Zdeno Chara hoists the Stanley Cup trophy after the team's Game 7 win against Vancouver at Rogers Arena. Stuart Cahill | Boston Herald

Above: Bruins center Gregory Campbell attempts to jam the puck in on Vancouver goalie Roberto Luongo during Game 7 at Rogers Arena.
Stuart Cahill | Boston Herald

"He's so deserving of everything he's gotten," coach Claude Julien said. "The one thing he did for our hockey club is every night with him in net, we knew we had a chance, no matter if we had a slow start. We always had a chance to (win) with Timmy."

Bergeron scored the first of his two goals at 14:37 of the first period off a nice feed from Marchand.

Then Marchand made it 2-0 at 12:13 of the

Above: Bruins left winger Brad Marchand wraps the puck around the pipe as Tampa Bay goalie Roberto Luongo is slow to react in Game 7 at Rogers Arena. *Stuart Cahill | Boston Herald*

Opposite Page: Bruins left winger Brad Marchand (63) celebrates his goal with teammates, including defenseman Zdeno Chara (center), during Game 7 at Rogers Arena. *Stuart Cahill | Boston Herald*

second. He took a loose puck away from Kevin Bieksa at the left side of the crease, carried it behind the net and jammed it past netminder Roberto Luongo.

Bergeron added his second of the game with 2:25 left in the middle period with a shorthanded goal. With Zdeno Chara off for interference, Dennis Seidenberg sent a pass up the middle for Bergeron. Canucks defenseman Christian Ehrhoff hauled Bergeron down and a penalty was going to be called, but after Luongo made the original save, the puck went off Bergeron and in. The play was reviewed, but the goal stood up.

After that, the only cheers given to Luongo, who will have to wait a long time before he lives down his critique of Thomas after Game 5, were of the mock variety.

It was only fitting for this squad that identified so much with the concept of team that it was its hardworking second line, which also shut down the Sedin twins in this series, that delivered the giant silver chalice.

"That whole line has been awesome," forward Chris Kelly said. "They started the game and they set the tone for us and we just followed. I thought we got contributions from everyone, but our big guys stepped up and played a big, big role (last night)."

The B's had lost a three-goal lead in Game 7 to the Philadelphia Flyers last year in the Eastern Conference semifinals, but they weren't about to let this one slip away. They frustrated the Canucks at every turn in the third period, even when Milan Lucic took a questionable hooking call with 8:26 left. But the B's killed it off with ease, as they did most of Vancouver's power plays in this series. The penalty-killing unit was an incredible 31-for-33 against a power play that was clicking at over 28 percent coming into the series.

Finally, after Luongo was pulled for an extra attacker with 3:10 left, Marchand took away any flickering hope when he snapped an

empty-netter home with 2:44 remaining. The trash-talking pretenders that the Canucks turned out to be were finished, and Marchand, no angel himself, basked in their defeat.

"They were diving, they hit (Nathan Horton) like that, they kept whining about stuff in the papers and shooting their mouths off," Marchand said. "We just took it, went with it and we just played our game."

And last night when they needed their game most, the Bruins just about played it to perfection.■

Bruins players surround the Stanley Cup after polishing off Vancouver in Game 7 of the finals at Rogers Arena. Christopher Evans | Boston Herald

By Steve Buckley

Though the Stanley Cup eluded them for 39 years, the Bruins still had big, tough guys whose very presence on the ice defined greatness.

They had the last days of Orr and Esposito and Bucyk, followed by O'Reilly, followed by Middleton, followed by Bourque, followed by Neely.

Yet when the Cup drought finally ended last night, the Bruins emerging from a deadly quiet Rogers Arena with a 4-0 victory over the Vancouver Canucks in the all-or-nothing Game 7, they were led not by great players but by players who played great.

To be sure, they benefited from the stellar goaltending of Conn Smythe Trophy winner Tim Thomas, who turned the finals into a one-man video on how to man the pipes in pressure situations, and who, in doing so, reduced Canucks goalie Roberto Luongo to forever soldiering on as The Man Who Dissed Timmy.

Look beyond Thomas, though, and it was a collection of hardscrabble, blue-collar hockey players - working stiffs - who turned the Boston bars and taverns upside down last night. Yes, Milan Lucic and Patrice Bergeron and David Krejci may one day be great. And Mark Recchi once was great. But once you get past the big fella on the blue line, Zdeno Chara, this ain't the Big, Bad Bruins. They're the Medium-Sized, Good Bruins.

And considering they are the 2010-11 Stanley Cup champions, that's good enough.

"You may not look at these guys and say that this guy or that guy is a superstar," said Cam Neely, finally part of a Cup winner in his role as team president. "We had some damned good players, really skilled players, but more importantly they played as a team and the depth was a big part of it."

Depth. Neely used that word a hundred times last night.

"You look at being able to roll four lines out there when the coach wanted to and had to and needed to," said Neely. "That's what depth is all about."

And how about that coach? The ongoing buzz during the Eastern Conference quarterfinals held that Claude Julien would get the gate if the Bruins didn't get past the Montreal Canadiens, right?

Yet here he is, a Cup-winning coach. And for those of you who wonder if the buttoned-up Julien is capable of lightening up, we have proof that, yes, he is. Asked last night to assess the performance of Thomas, Julien replied, "He (stunk)."

But if Julien has risen on the coaching depth chart in the eyes of Boston sports fans, the coach himself has a collection of players who have risen on his depth chart. Consider Brad Marchand, a 23-year-old rookie who was strictly fourth-line fill when training camp began but who worked himself up the lines during the season, and then, in the Stanley Cup finals, worked himself into the nightmares of the Canucks and their fans.

Last night, in the biggest game of his life, Marchand had two goals and an assist.

Is this something Julien saw coming?

"Absolutely, totally not," Julien said. "He was a first-year player. But the impact he had on our team is way, way beyond what we expected of him. But that's what makes championship teams, guys that come out and give you more than you expected."

Can we add Patrice Bergeron to that list? When he suffered a concussion in the last game of the second-round series with the Philadelphia Flyers, the fear was that he'd be lost for the remainder of the playoffs. He had two goals last night in the biggest of games.

How about defenseman Dennis Seidenberg? In September 2009, he was casting about for work when he hooked on with the Florida Panthers. In March 2010, he was traded to the Bruins. In June 2011, he picked up two assists in Game 7 of the Stanley Cup finals.

How about Tyler Seguin answering the bell when Bergeron got hurt? How about Shawn Thornton dusting himself off and, in addition to providing muscle, giving fourth-line oomph?

"Regardless of whether we won or not, this was still going to be one of the best groups I ever played with," said the retiring Recchi, who played on three Cup winners with three different teams in three different decades. "We were committed right from the get-go."

For years, the Bruins were classic underachievers at best, out-of-the-postseason laughingstocks at worst. They deserved all the criticism that came their way.

Nobody's laughing now.

The Bruins are champions, and we have to ask: When are the Patriots, Red Sox and Celtics going to join them?■

Above: Mark Recchi fills the cup as Zdeno Chara sprays his back with champagne while celebrating at Rogers Arena after the Bruins' Game 7 triumph against Vancouver. Christopher Evans | Boston Herald

Bruins center Patrice Bergeron kisses the Stanley Cup after the team's Game 7 win against Vancouver at Rogers Arena.   Christopher Evans | Boston Herald